Writing from Within

Curtis Kelly & Arlen Gargagliano

CAMBRIDGE
UNIVERSITY PRESS

CAMBRIDGE UNIVERSITY PRESS
Cambridge, New York, Melbourne, Madrid, Cape Town, Singapore, São Paulo, Delhi

Cambridge University Press
32 Avenue of the Americas, New York, NY 10013–2473, USA

www.cambridge.org
Information on this title: www.cambridge.org/9780521626828

First published 2001
16th printing 2008

Printed in Hong Kong, China, by Golden Cup Printing Company Limited

A catalog record for this publication is available from the British Library

ISBN 978-0-521-62682-8 student's book
ISBN 978-0-521-62681-1 teacher's manual

Illustrations: Kathryn Adams – 4,5,10 *(bottom)*, 20, 30–31, 44, 55, 59, 61, 71, 74–75, 78, 80,
96 *(bottom)*, 103, 108, 119; Leila Cabib – 9, 10 *(top)*, 16, 21, 25, 28, 35, 42, 58, 62, 66, 68, 88,
91, 101, 105, 112, 116; Lynn Fellman/Fellman Studio Inc. – 6 *(bottom)*, 13-14, 34, 39, 43, 49,
51, 64, 69, 83, 85, 87, 92–93, 106, 109, 114; Stanford Kay/Paragraphics – 8, 17, 29, 36–38, 48,
54, 72, 81, 90, 110, 118; Otto Steininger – 6 *(top)*, 7, 23, 26, 33, 52, 56, 99, 117.

Book design, art direction, and layout services: Adventure House, NYC

Contents

Plan of the book

Unit	Title	Prewriting
1	About me	☐ main ideas ☐ general and specific information ☐ topic sentences
2	Career consultant	☐ logical organization 1 ☐ inference sentences
3	A dream come true	☐ facts and examples in paragraphs ☐ supporting sentences
4	Invent!	☐ definition paragraphs ☐ attention getters
5	It changed my life!	☐ cause-and-effect paragraphs ☐ introductory paragraphs
6	Exciting destinations	☐ process paragraphs ☐ guidebook style
7	Research survey	☐ classification style ☐ concluding paragraphs
8	The power interview	☐ comparison-contrast paragraphs ☐ expressions that show contrast
9	Personal goals	☐ persuasive paragraphs ☐ parallelism ☐ sentence transitions
10	Architect	☐ logical organization 2 ☐ topic division
11	My role models	☐ paragraph links
12	Be a reporter	☐ newspaper styles ☐ headlines

Writing	Editing	Option
☐ writing a paragraph about things I like to do	☐ paragraph format	☐ writing a paragraph about myself
☐ writing a composition about career choice	☐ sentence connectors	☐ writing a letter requesting information
☐ writing a magazine article about a classmate	☐ direct and indirect speech	☐ writing a resume
☐ writing a composition about an invention	☐ pronouns	☐ writing a letter to a company about a product
☐ writing a composition about an important day	☐ cause-and-effect words	☐ designing a greeting card
☐ writing a guidebook article about a one-day tour	☐ modifiers	☐ writing a letter requesting tourist information
☐ writing a research report	☐ commas	☐ researching restaurants and creating a restaurant guide
☐ writing a magazine article about interviewing techniques	☐ ways of giving advice	☐ reporting on interview results
☐ writing a letter to myself about goals	☐ incomplete sentences	☐ writing about classmates and finding out about myself
☐ writing a composition about dormitory design	☐ articles	☐ designing a dormitory poster
☐ writing a composition about an important person	☐ subject-verb agreement	☐ writing a letter to someone who has influenced me
☐ writing a newspaper article	☐ other words for *said*	☐ writing a letter to my teacher

We, the authors of *Writing from Within*, believe that the greatest hurdle our student writers must face is learning how to organize their writing. Therefore, the main focus of this text is teaching them how to generate topics, write cohesive paragraphs, and organize them into clear, logical expository compositions. We focus on expository writing – or explaining – because it uses an organizational style that differs from the styles used in other languages, and also because it represents the kind of writing our learners will have to do in academic or business environments.

We also believe that excellence in student writing goes beyond mere accuracy or the ability to mimic models. Excellence comes from writing that leads to discovery of self, of ideas, and of others, and self-expression is its own reward. Students should be pulled into learning through interesting and expressive activities rather than be pushed into learning through fear of failure. Therefore, we have chosen to offer writing topics that will challenge your learners' creativity, lead them to introspection, and most important, allow them to experience writing as a joyful exertion.

The focus of each unit is a writing assignment. Some are introspective: For example, learners are asked to reflect on a major life event that has led to growth. Others are more conventional but task-based: Learners are asked to plan a trip abroad and to publish a class newspaper. In this way, humanistic writing assignments are interleaved with task-based writing assignments, providing a broad range of writing experiences. In addition, each unit ends with an optional expansion activity that gives each learner an opportunity to communicate with an outside party.

Each unit offers learners different organizational tools, which are practiced in prewriting exercises. Learners are trained in using a variety of expository modes, such as Division, Classification, and Cause and Effect. Editing skills are taught by giving learners practice in mechanics and grammar. Each unit takes 3–5 hours of class time to complete, and although the syllabus is developmental, it is not necessary to do each unit in order.

At the center of each unit (with the exception of Unit 1) is a composition assignment. The lessons that come before the composition assignment are prewriting activities, in which students generate content and organize it. The lessons that come after the writing assignment are revision, feedback, and expansion activities.

Prewriting	Brainstorming	The topic is introduced and writing ideas are generated.
	Paragraph analysis	Students analyze a model paragraph.
	Organizational practice	Students learn expository organizational skills and learn how to organize their compositions.

Writing	Model and assignment	*Students analyze a model and receive instructions for writing their compositions.*
Postwriting	Editing	*Students correct grammatical errors common to beginning writers and edit their compositions.*
	Giving feedback	*Students exchange compositions with other students for review and feedback.*
	Option	*Almost a separate unit in itself, the optional writing activity helps students transfer their newly gained skills to a real communicative writing task.*

Writing is a skill. We tell our students that learning to write is like learning to play a musical instrument; the more they practice, the better they will be. *Writing from Within* is designed to demonstrate to learners that they have the knowledge within themselves to develop this skill. We hope they will enjoy this text, and we look forward to hearing your comments.

Curtis Kelly
Arlen Gargagliano

Acknowledgments

Writing is a process. In this case, *Writing from Within* was a process that spanned years and continents. The authors wish to thank the numerous people who helped in the development of this project. Particular thanks are owed to the following:

The insights and suggestions of the teachers who reviewed and piloted **Writing from Within** *and helped define the content of this book:* Bruce Benson, **Shoin Women's College**, Nara, Japan; Nick Brideson, **Global Village Language Center**, Taipei, Taiwan; Martin Willis, **Tokyo Women's Christian University**, Tokyo, Japan; Sally Gearheart, **Santa Rosa Junior College**, Santa Rosa, California, USA; Michael Kastner, **Hanyang University**, Seoul, Korea; John Hedgcock, **Monterey Institute of International Studies**, Monterey, California, USA; Chris Bunn, **City College**, San Francisco, California, USA; Kathy Sherak, **San Francisco State University**, San Francisco, California, USA.

Additional thanks are owed to the following: Kathleen Schultz, Diane Frangie, Linda Donan, Nathan Furuya, Elizabeth Hizer, Trenton Jones, Eric Sheldon, Ian Shortreed, John Gebhardt, Frank Carter, Scott Dantonio, Paul Kelley, Vicki Starfire, Randy Terhune, Bill Essig, Nobuhiro Adachi, Phil Jordan, Lynda Dalgish, Patricia Capobianco, Teresa Starr, Caroline Coppola, David Bernstein, and especially our families, without whose patience, love, and support this project would not have been completed.

The editorial and production team: Sylvia P. Bloch, David Bohlke, Liane Carita, Mary Carson, Dee E. Davis, Ann Dickson, Deborah Goldblatt, Nada Gordon, Margot Gramer, Sharon Lee, James R. Morgan, Kathy Niemczyk, Howard Siegelman, Mary Vaughn, and Jennifer Wilkin.

And Cambridge University Press staff and advisors: Kathleen Corley, Steve Golden, Nigel McQuitty, Mark O'Neil, Andrew Robinson, Dan Schulte, and Janaka Williams.

Preview

1. Work with a partner. Write the answer to this question.

What is a paragraph?

_____

_____

2. Look at the bottom of page 3 to check your answer.

3. Now read the two paragraphs below, and follow the instructions.

> ### Movies
>
> There are three reasons why I love movies. First of all, movies take us all over the world. We can see beautiful sights and learn about interesting cultures without ever leaving home. Second, movies show us how other people live and solve their problems. This helps us make decisions about our own problems. Finally, and maybe most important, movies are just plain fun. After a hard day at work, it feels good to sit down and be entertained by a good movie.

> ### Television
>
> My family has three television sets. Some channels are in languages other than English, so I can't watch them. I like TV because there are so many different shows, but I don't like to watch television with my brother because he changes the channels all the time. Some people like comedies because they help us forget a hard day at work. As for me, I like news and music shows the best. Some shows are very funny, and some teach us about foreign countries and cultures.

a. Which paragraph is easier to understand because it's better organized? Circle one.

Movies   *Television*

If you said *Movies* is better organized, you are right!

b. *Movies* is better organized because it has only one topic. Circle its topic.

travel movies   *what kinds of movies are best*   *why I like movies*

c. *Movies* has a topic sentence. The topic sentence gives the main idea of the paragraph. Underline the topic sentence in the paragraph.

d. *Movies* uses transition words and phrases such as *first of all* to connect ideas in the paragraph. Find the other two transition words in the paragraph. Circle them.

In this book, you will gain the knowledge and skills necessary to write paragraphs. Now, take a moment to read how this book can help you do this.

One of the main purposes of writing is to communicate with others. When non-native speakers write in English, however, they may have trouble communicating. Their writing may be hard to understand. Students may think they do not know enough grammar or vocabulary to write well, but this is not necessarily the case. They often have trouble communicating in written English because their organization is weak.

By using this book you will learn how to organize your writing so that it is easier to understand. Your ability to communicate in written English will improve.

When you write something, you gain knowledge. This is because when you write about a topic, you have to think about it carefully. As you do this, you come to understand your subject better and even discover new things about it. This new understanding of your subject may cause you to write something different from what you thought you would.

We would like you to discover new things about yourself. This is why so many of the writing assignments in this text focus on you and your experiences. By writing about yourself — your life and way of thinking — you will understand yourself better. We firmly believe that "writing from within" is a way to gain knowledge about yourself.

Curtis Kelly
Arlen Gargagliano

A paragraph
- is a section of writing about a single idea.
- contains at least one sentence but usually several sentences.

The first sentence of a paragraph
- begins on a new line.
- starts to the right of the other sentences.

Unit **1** *About me*

| Lesson 1 | **What is brainstorming?** |

Brainstorming

When you brainstorm, you write as many words or phrases as you can think of about a topic. You don't have to write complete sentences when brainstorming.

1. Whenever you brainstorm, think about whether you can break something down into smaller parts.

For example, while brainstorming about "Things I like to do," imagine you wrote down "drawing pictures." How could you break this idea down further?

<u>drawing pictures</u>

– of airplanes   – of cars
– of people   – of animals

2. Now look at these brainstorming notes. Notice the smaller parts, or subtopics. Can you add a few more ideas?

<u>Things I like to do</u>

<u>traveling</u>
    -beach
    -mountains
    -interesting cities
    -_____

<u>using my computer</u>
    -making greeting cards
    -using the Internet
    -sending e-mail
    -_____

<u>shopping</u>
    -buying computer software
        -computer games
        -graphics software
    -buying magazines
        -Internet magazines
        -computer magazines
    -_____
    -_____

3. Now brainstorm for three minutes about things you like to do. Write at least 15 things.

Things I like to do

go to the park down the street

4. Compare lists with a partner. How many things are similar? How many are different?

Using ideas from your partner's list, can you add additional information to your own list?

Later in this unit . . .

You will write a paragraph about things you like to do.

You will learn to identify and write phrases with general and specific information. You will also learn what makes a good topic sentence.

1. Read the paragraph below and follow the instructions.

My Worries
There are many things that worry me, but the most common ones are being on time, getting my homework done, and saving money. I worry about being on time because I don't like to make other people wait, and I don't like to miss anything. I always try to arrive a little early. I also worry about getting my homework done. After school, I go to my part-time job and don't get home until about eight o'clock. That gives me only one or two hours to do my homework, and I'm usually too tired to do a good job. I worry about saving money, too. I'm trying to save enough money to go to England this summer, but I haven't saved very much so far. I go out with my friends too often and spend more than I should. I will have to either stop spending so much money or forget about my summer plans.

a. What is the main idea of this paragraph? Write one to four words.

_____

b. What sentence states the main idea of the paragraph? Underline it above.

c. What are the specific details the author uses to explain the main idea?
Finish the sentences.

1. I worry about _being on time_____

because _____

_____.

2. I worry about _____

because _____

_____.

3. I worry about _____

because _____

_____.

2. Compare answers with a partner.

Learning about
organization

Look at the lists of general information and specific information.

General information		Specific information
sports	⟶	volleyball
shopping	⟶	buying hiking boots
TV shows	⟶	sitcoms
things that irritate me	⟶	people talking during movies

1. Study the examples. In each column, one phrase has general information (**G**) and three phrases have specific information (**S**).

a
_G_ things that irritate me
_S_ late trains
_S_ rude waiters
_S_ barking dogs

b
_S_ jog daily
_S_ do aerobics
_G_ how to stay in shape
_S_ avoid junk food

c
_S_ free concerts
_G_ advantages of New York
_S_ interesting people
_S_ excellent museums

2. Look at these lists. In each column, which phrase is general and which phrases are specific? Write one **G** and three **S**s in the blanks.

a
___ action dramas
___ sitcoms
___ good shows on TV
___ news programs

b
___ popular software
___ word-processing
   software
___ spreadsheet software
___ Internet software

c
___ learning about another
   culture
___ good reasons to have
   an international
   pen pal
___ improving your English
   writing skills
___ making a friend abroad

3. Now complete these lists with your own ideas. There should be one general (**G**) and three specific (**S**) groups of words.

a
G _music that I like_
S _____
S _____
S _____

b
G _bad habits_
S _____
S _____
S _____

c
G _____
S _driving a car_
S _taking the train_
S _walking_

4. Compare answers with a partner.

*Paragraphs usually have **topic sentences**. A topic sentence is very useful for organizing a paragraph because it states what the entire paragraph is about. A good topic sentence should be a general sentence that presents the topic clearly.*

1. Read each paragraph below. Mark the best topic sentence with a **T**.

> *My car always smells like exhaust fumes. I've had two flat tires this year. Sometimes it won't even start in the morning.*

a. ___ My car smells, has flat tires, and won't start.

b. ___ So it's time to get a new car.

c. _T_ I have a lot of trouble with my car.

> Thirty years ago, magnetic tape was used only to record music and voices. Later, it was also used to record computer programs and data. The biggest use today, however, is for videotape recording.

d. ___ The uses of magnetic tape have greatly increased.

e. ___ Magnetic tape is good.

f. ___ Magnetic tape has been used with computers.

> *A long time ago, the apple was a symbol of forbidden knowledge because of the story of the Garden of Eden in the Bible. Later, it became a traditional gift for teachers. These days, many people think of the computer company with the same name when they hear the word "apple."*

g. ___ Apples taste good, too.

h. ___ The apple has been a symbol of many things.

i. ___ An apple represents forbidden knowledge because of the Bible, school because it was a traditional gift, and a computer company because it has the same name.

2. Compare answers with a partner. Did you agree on the topic sentences?

3. With your partner, discuss the reasons the other sentences are not good topic sentences. Mark each sentence with one of these reasons.

G It is too general.
S It contains too much specific information.
C It makes a concluding statement.
N It is not related to the other sentences.
P It is a summary of only part of the paragraph.

General and specific information

1. Choose three items on your brainstorming list from page 5. For each item, write one phrase that contains general information and three phrases that contain specific information. Look at the example.

G *three places I like to go to*
S *the Thai Orchid Restaurant*
S *Powell's Bookstore*
S *the park down the street*

a

G _____

S _____

S _____

S _____

b

G _____

S _____

S _____

S _____

c

G _____

S _____

S _____

S _____

2. Now write a topic sentence for each of the items in Exercise 1.

Near my apartment, there are three places that I like to go to.

a. _____

b. _____

c. _____

3. Choose a, b, or c to write a paragraph about in Lesson 6. Circle the letter.

1. Read the paragraph below and follow the instructions.

> ### Three Special Places
> Near my apartment, there are three places I like to go to. The first is the Thai Orchid Restaurant. Thai food is my favorite kind of food, and the chef there is excellent. The restaurant isn't too expensive, so I often go there with my friends. It's a nice place to relax, talk, and enjoy a delicious meal. The second place is Powell's Bookstore. Powell's is one of the biggest bookstores in my city, so I can find books on almost any subject there. The people who work there are very friendly. If I can't find a book, they will gladly order it for me. The third place I like to go to is the park down the street from my apartment. It has huge trees and a beautiful garden. I sometimes go there after eating a fine Thai meal, and I sit under a tree to read a book from Powell's.

a. What is the main idea of the paragraph? Circle it.

Thai food   places I like   reading in the park

b. Underline the topic sentence.

c. Subtopics are parts of the main topic. There are three subtopics in the paragraph above. Write them here.

_____   _____   _____

2. Compare answers with a partner.

3. Now write a similar paragraph, using the topic you chose in Lesson 5. Underline the topic sentence.

Paragraph 1 uses an incorrect format. Paragraph 2 is correct.

1

Start the first line of the paragraph a little to the right of the other lines. It should start about five spaces to the right.
Write to the end of every line except the last one.
If a sentence ends in the middle of the line, don't go down to the next line to start the next sentence. Start it on the same line.

2

Start the first line of the paragraph a little to the right of the other lines. It should start about five spaces to the right. Write to the end of every line except the last one. If a sentence ends in the middle of the line, don't go down to the next line to start the next sentence. Start it on the same line.

1. Look at the two short paragraphs below. Each one has mistakes in format. Rewrite them without the mistakes.

I spend most of my day at work. In the morning I read letters from customers and write down their questions.
Then, in the afternoon, I call these customers and answer their questions.

At home, I spend a lot of time on the Internet. I find the Internet useful in two ways. I can keep in touch with my friends by sending e-mail messages, and I can also do research for my job.

2. Compare answers with a partner. Did you rewrite the paragraphs in the same way?

3. Now look at the paragraph you wrote in Lesson 6. Did you use correct paragraph format?

What do you think?

Giving feedback

1. Show a partner your paragraph from Lesson 6. Read your partner's paragraph. Then answer the questions.

a. Did the author include a topic sentence? Circle one.   Yes   No

b. Did the author underline the topic sentence? Circle one.   Yes   No

c. Write your partner's topic sentence here. _____

_____

d. Write another possible topic sentence for the paragraph.

_____

_____

e. Can you find any subtopics? What are they? Write them here.

_____   _____   _____

2. Do you like to do the same kinds of things as your partner? Write a short note to your partner saying why or why not. Look at the examples.

Dear Andrea,

You and I are very similar. I also like going to the beach, playing volleyball, and listening to music. I think we're both summer people!

Your friend,
Chris

Dear Jonathan,

I think we're very different. You like hiking, playing basketball, and riding your bicycle, but I don't. You're much more active than I am!

See you,
Emily

3. Show your note to your partner.

1. Write another paragraph about yourself. Choose one of these topics, or use your own idea.

- *things I like to do*
- *places I like to go to*
- *people I like*
- *things I am good at*
- _____

2. Follow the instructions below.

   a. Don't write your name on the paper, and don't show it to anyone.

   b. When you finish, give your paper to your teacher. Your teacher will write numbers on the papers and place them around the room.

3. Read the papers and guess which classmate wrote each paragraph. Make a list.

Paragraph number	Author
1	
2	
3	
4	
5	
6	
7	
8	

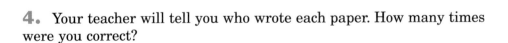

4. Your teacher will tell you who wrote each paper. How many times were you correct?

Unit 2 Career consultant

Brainstorming

1. Think about your personality type. What are some things you like? What do you dislike? Brainstorm for three minutes and make two lists.

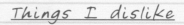

Things I like

eating ice cream
being alone

Things I dislike

doing homework
repairing things

2. Compare lists with a partner. Do you like or dislike any of the same things?

3. Now imagine you are looking for a job. Think about your own personality and things you like to do. What kinds of jobs would be appropriate for you? Write two possibilities here.

_____   _____

4. Compare answers with a partner.

Later in this unit . . .

You will write a composition and suggest a job for someone.

You will also learn about organizing your ideas logically, making inference sentences, and connecting sentences.

Organizing ideas logically

I. Read the paragraph below and follow the instructions.

Your Career and Personal Style

Think about it. You will probably spend more time at work than anywhere else. Of course, you should choose a career according to your interests, but shouldn't you also try to find a career that fits your personality? Understanding the three parts of your "personal style" might help when you decide on a career. First, are you more interested in having friends or being successful? For example, in your free time do you usually meet your friends or do your homework first? Second, are you more active or passive? Do you prefer to talk or to listen when you are with others? Do you prefer to be a decision maker or to be part of the group? Third, are you more of an emotional or a logical person? For instance, do you like to think through problems step by step or simply decide what to do according to your overall feeling about the situation at hand? In conclusion, in addition to thinking about your interests, it is also very important to consider your personality when choosing a career.

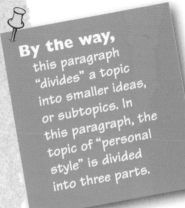

By the way, this paragraph "divides" a topic into smaller ideas, or subtopics. In this paragraph, the topic of "personal style" is divided into three parts.

a. Underline the topic sentence.

b. Three subtopics follow the topic sentence. Circle them.

c. The concluding sentence summarizes the main points of the paragraph. It is often introduced by a transition word or phrase such as *in summary*, *in conclusion*, or *finally*. What is the concluding sentence? Circle it.

d. What are the other transition words? Write them in the correct column.

Transition words that show the beginning of a new subtopic	**Transition words that provide more specific information on the same subtopic**
First,	*For example,*

2. Compare answers with a partner.

Inference sentences

*An **inference sentence** is one type of topic sentence. It is a logical conclusion based on the information found in the paragraph's supporting sentences.*

1. In each of the following groups of sentences about job choices and personality, one sentence is an inference sentence and the rest are supporting sentences.

Check (✔) the inference sentence. Look at the example.

- ◻ Seeing blood or injuries doesn't bother Marta.
- ◻ Marta enjoys taking care of people.
- ◻ Marta is interested in biology and chemistry.
- ✔ A career in medicine would be good for Marta.

a
- ◻ Sandy likes to write lists before making decisions.
- ◻ Sandy likes to solve problems step by step.
- ◻ Sandy would make a better scientist than artist.
- ◻ Sandy is very good at math.

b
- ◻ Being a writer seems like a good career for Akemi.
- ◻ Akemi prefers working alone to working with others.
- ◻ Akemi loves to read novels, poetry, and short stories.
- ◻ Akemi likes to observe people.

c
- ◻ Joe reads fashion magazines to learn about the latest fashion trends.
- ◻ Joe likes to draw his own clothing patterns.
- ◻ The job of fashion designer would be perfect for Joe.
- ◻ Joe enjoys sewing.
- ◻ Joe is very creative.

d
- ◻ David likes loud parties.
- ◻ David has many friends.
- ◻ David would rather be in a crowded place than an empty place.
- ◻ David has a people-oriented personality.
- ◻ A career in sales would suit David.

e
- ◻ Mimi dislikes puzzles and board games.
- ◻ One of Mimi's hobbies is gardening.
- ◻ Mimi likes to take part in sports rather than just watch them.
- ◻ Mimi seems to prefer physical activities to mental activities.
- ◻ Mimi's favorite class at school is Dance.

f
- ◻ Carol always reads the financial section of the newspaper.
- ◻ The job of stockbroker would be ideal for Carol.
- ◻ One of Carol's ambitions is to make a lot of money.
- ◻ Carol likes to take risks.
- ◻ Carol is very good with numbers.

2. Compare answers with a partner.

1. Take turns using these questions to interview your partner about his or her personal style. Later, this information will help you find an ideal career for your partner.

a. What are four things you like to do?

_____   _____

_____   _____

b. What are two of your strengths? For example, are you good at solving problems? physically strong? artistic? patient?

_____   _____

2. What does your partner prefer in a job? Look at the example. Then interview your partner and complete the chart.

Do you prefer working alone or with others?

I prefer working alone.

I prefer working with others.

I'm not sure. I like both equally.

1	working alone	working with others	not sure/like both equally
2	making less money but having more free time	making more money but having less free time	not sure/like both equally
3	talking to others	thinking by oneself	not sure/like both equally
4	being logical	emphasizing feelings	not sure/like both equally
5	doing physical activities	doing mental activities	not sure/like both equally
6	working indoors	working outdoors	not sure/like both equally
7	taking risks	being cautious	not sure/like both equally
8	having a flexible schedule	having a fixed schedule	not sure/like both equally
9	being active	being passive	not sure/like both equally

Job placement chart

1. Look at the chart below. Then look back at the responses your partner gave in Lesson 4. Check your partner's responses in the chart where they appear. If your partner chose *not sure/like both equally*, don't write anything.

For example, if your partner prefers . . .

I	✔ working alone	☐ working with others	☐ not sure/like both equally	

then check (✔) *working alone* in the chart below *Tour guides* and *Architects* like this:

	Tour guides should like . . .	Bank employees should like . . .	Architects should like . . .	Sales representatives should like . . .
I	✔ working alone	☐ working with others	✔ working alone	☐ working with others

Now fill in the chart using your partner's responses. Write the total number of checks in the spaces provided at the bottom of the chart.

	Tour guides should like . . .	Bank employees should like . . .	Architects should like . . .	Sales representatives should like . . .
I	☐ working alone	☐ working with others	☐ working alone	☐ working with others
2	☐ making less money but having more free time	☐ making more money but having less free time	☐ making less money but having more free time	☐ making more money but having less free time
3	☐ talking to others	☐ thinking by oneself	☐ thinking by oneself	☐ talking to others
4	☐ emphasizing feelings	☐ being logical	☐ being logical	☐ emphasizing feelings
5	☐ doing physical activities	☐ doing mental activities	☐ doing mental activities	☐ doing physical activities
6	☐ working outdoors	☐ working indoors	☐ working outdoors	☐ working indoors
7	☐ taking risks	☐ being cautious	☐ being cautious	☐ taking risks
8	☐ having a flexible schedule	☐ having a fixed schedule	☐ having a fixed schedule	☐ having a flexible schedule
9	☐ being active	☐ being passive	☐ being passive	☐ being active
Total				

2. Which job has the most checks? This is the job that suits your partner the best. Write it here.

_____

3. Now think of a job not listed here that you think would suit your partner. Don't ask your partner – think of one yourself. Write it here.

_____

1. You are going to write a composition about an appropriate job for your partner. Use the job you chose in Lesson 5, or choose another one.

2. Read the example composition and follow the instructions.

> *A Future Teacher*
>
> *Claudia has a wonderful personality. There are so many things that she would be good at, but if I had to choose one job for her, it would be elementary school teacher.*
>
> *First of all, Claudia likes people. She enjoys talking to others and seems to make friends easily. She's good at telling jokes and stories. Most important, she says that she enjoys being with young children and cares about them very much. I think she would make a good teacher because of these qualities.*
>
> *Second, Claudia is very sensitive. She is the first person to notice if someone is sad or not feeling well, and she always tries to cheer that person up. Since children don't always say how they feel, her sensitivity would make her a good teacher.*
>
> *Finally, Claudia is well organized. She always has her appointments neatly scheduled on her calendar. Children need to follow a regular schedule, too. Therefore, I think Claudia would be a good teacher.*

a. Finish the sentence about your partner.

I think _____ would
　　　　　　　(name)

make a good _____ .
　　　　　　　　　　(job)

b. List three reasons for suggesting this job. Each reason should be explained in a separate paragraph. Write a word or a short phrase.

First reason

Second reason

Third reason

3. Now write a topic sentence for each of your reasons.

_____

_____

_____

_____

_____

4. Finally, put the parts together and write a composition. Underline the topic sentence in each paragraph.

You can use the conjunctions and, but, *and* so *to connect sentences.*

> John danced. His friend sang a song. ⟶ John danced, and his friend sang a song.

It is often not necessary to repeat the subject when both sentences have the same one.

> John danced. John sang a song. ⟶ John danced and sang a song.

But *and* so *usually have a comma in front of them. Sometimes* and *does, too.*

> John can speak Chinese, but he can't write it well.
> John wasn't feeling well, so the teacher sent him home early.

Do not use and, but, *or* so *to begin a sentence. Use these transition words instead.*

> and ⟶ **in addition / furthermore / also**
> but ⟶ **however / on the other hand**
> so ⟶ **therefore / as a result**
> John often works late. In addition, he sometimes works weekends.

1. Read the paragraph below. Add conjunctions and transition words to improve it. Cross out any word you would like to replace, and write the new word(s) above it.

> *In addition,*
> Yuki is a hard worker. ~~And~~ she is able to finish her work independently. For example, we had a group project to do in our economics class last year. There were three people in Yuki's group. But at the end of the first semester, both of her partners transferred to other schools. So she had to do the project by herself. She worked on it in the morning. She worked on it at lunchtime. She worked on it at night. Most people in that situation would have gone to the teacher and asked for help. But Yuki finished the project by herself. And it was one of the best in the class. Yuki does quality work. I believe she would make an excellent sales representative.

2. Now look at the composition you wrote in Lesson 6. Would similar changes improve it?

1. Read your partner's composition about you, and follow the instructions below.

a. What career does your partner suggest for you? Write it here.

_____

b. What are the three reasons your partner gives for suggesting this career? Write them here.

1. _____

2. _____

3. _____

2. Do you think the suggestion is a good one? Read the example and then write a short letter to your partner explaining why you agree or disagree with the choice.

> Dear Lucinda,
>
> I liked your suggestion that I become an elementary school teacher. I agree with you. I am a people-oriented person and have always wanted to do something that helps others.
> However, I think I would make one change to your suggestion. Instead of teaching elementary school students, I would prefer to teach adults. Maybe I will go to graduate school and get a degree in English.
> Anyway, thank you for your positive comments and encouragement. I was very pleased to read what you wrote.
>
> Sincerely,
> Claudia

By the way, this format is used for informal letters. See the next page for a format that is used for more formal business letters.

1. Find someone who does a job you are interested in. Write that person a letter to ask for advice. Follow these suggestions for writing your letter:

- ■ Introduce yourself.
- ■ Ask for the information politely. Show that you think this person is an expert.
- ■ List three points about yourself, and ask if this kind of job would be good for you.
- ■ Give generous thanks for the help.
- ■ Don't forget to sign your name.

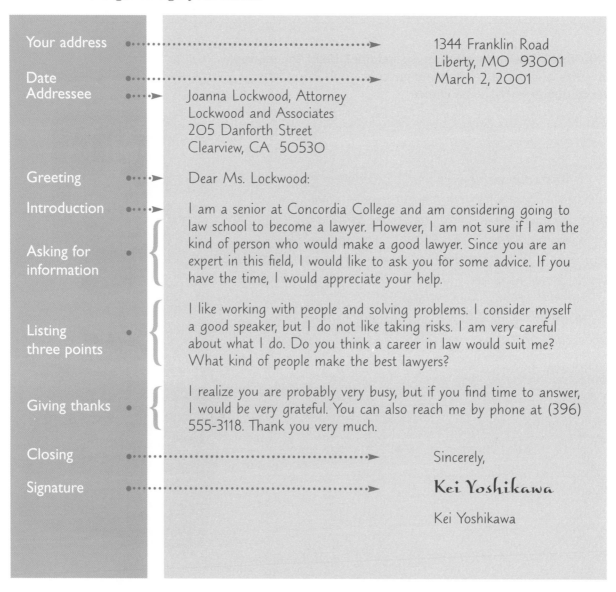

Your address	1344 Franklin Road
	Liberty, MO 93001
Date	March 2, 2001
Addressee	Joanna Lockwood, Attorney
	Lockwood and Associates
	205 Danforth Street
	Clearview, CA 50530
Greeting	Dear Ms. Lockwood:
Introduction	I am a senior at Concordia College and am considering going to law school to become a lawyer. However, I am not sure if I am the kind of person who would make a good lawyer. Since you are an expert in this field, I would like to ask you for some advice. If you have the time, I would appreciate your help.
Asking for information	
Listing three points	I like working with people and solving problems. I consider myself a good speaker, but I do not like taking risks. I am very careful about what I do. Do you think a career in law would suit me? What kind of people make the best lawyers?
Giving thanks	I realize you are probably very busy, but if you find time to answer, I would be very grateful. You can also reach me by phone at (396) 555-3118. Thank you very much.
Closing	Sincerely,
Signature	*Kei Yoshikawa*
	Kei Yoshikawa

2. When you finish, send the letter. Be sure to send a thank-you note if you get a reply.

Unit 3 — A dream come true

Lesson 1 — Success

1. What do you need to do to become successful? What characteristics do you need? Brainstorm for three minutes and make two lists.

> _What I need to do_
>
> graduate from college
>
>
> _Characteristics I need_
>
> diligence
> intelligence

2. Compare lists with a partner. Are there any additional items you want to add to your lists?

3. Circle the most important thing you need to do or the most important characteristic you need to have in order to be successful.

Later in this unit . . .

You will write about a successful person.

You will also learn about supporting sentences as well as direct and indirect speech.

1. Read the paragraph below and follow the instructions.

A Great Leader

Imagine a place where people are judged not "by the color of their skin but by the content of their character." These words were the dream of the civil rights leader Dr. Martin Luther King, Jr. To make his dream come true, he spent his life fighting racism and prejudice in the United States. He played several roles in his fight for equal rights for all Americans. First, he was a pastor in a church. He disliked violence and taught his congregation that they could win the war of inequality with love, not hate. Besides being a pastor, he was also a speaker. His "I Have a Dream" speech is still considered one of the best speeches of the twentieth century. Furthermore, he was a group organizer. He traveled throughout the South helping African Americans register to vote, and he organized a huge march on Washington, D.C. King said that he wanted to change the United States and, in many ways, he succeeded. Consequently, many Americans consider him a great leader.

By the way,
this paragraph uses facts and examples to support its main points. Use this style when your topic is hard to define or when you need strong support for the main idea.

a. Underline the topic sentence.

b. What three facts support the topic sentence? Write them here.

1. *He was a pastor who believed in love.* _____

2. _____

3. _____

c. What is the concluding sentence? Circle it.

d. Two things that Dr. King said are written in this paragraph. Write **D** for *direct speech* above the exact quote. Write **I** for *indirect speech* above an explanation of his words.

2. Compare answers with a partner.

Facts and examples can help support a topic sentence.

Topic sentence: *Tiger Woods is one of the best athletes in the world.*
Supporting sentence: *He is the youngest person to win the Masters golf tournament.*
Supporting sentence: *He spent two years developing a new golf swing.*

1. First, complete each topic sentence. Then write two sentences to support it.

Topic sentence:	_____ is an excellent fashion designer.
Supporting sentence:	_____
Supporting sentence:	_____

Topic sentence:	One of the best filmmakers is _____.
Supporting sentence:	_____
Supporting sentence:	_____

Topic sentence:	I think the most talented _____ is _____.
Supporting sentence:	_____
Supporting sentence:	_____

Topic sentence:	A very successful person I know is _____.
Supporting sentence:	_____
Supporting sentence:	_____

2. Compare answers with a partner.

Lesson 4 Looking back on your life

Prewriting

1. What is your greatest dream? Do you dream about becoming an award-winning designer? a pilot? a doctor? Write a sentence about your dream.

____

____

2. Imagine that ten years have passed and your dream has come true. First, look at the example about the professional director. Then complete the chart below it with the key events of your own life.

Today's date: *May 25, 2012*

What I am today: *a professional director*

Year	Key events in my rise to success:
2001	graduated from college
2003	won a nationwide film contest
2004	moved to Los Angeles
2005	entered film school

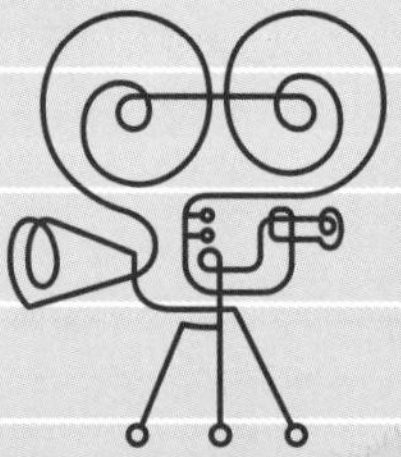

Today's date: ______________________

What I am today: ______________________

Year	Key events in my rise to success:

How successful are you?

1. Imagine you are a magazine reporter. Interview your partner about the details of his or her climb to success. Ask questions like the ones below, and take notes.

What are you doing today? What are some of your successes?

How did you become so successful? Please be specific.

2. Write two *actual* characteristics that helped make your partner successful. Here are some examples.

humorous	sincere	compassionate	intelligent
hardworking	sensible	creative	determined

Characteristics: _____   _____

3. Now write two sentences about your partner – one that describes him or her and one that supports your observations.

Jun-Ho is intelligent and a good observer. He often notices things that

other people do not.

1. You are going to write a magazine article based on the interview with your partner in Lesson 5. First, read the example article and follow the instructions.

First paragraph

> Jun-Ho: Award-Winning Director
> Jun-Ho is the most popular film director alive. His movies are enjoyed by both young and old. His topics are interesting, and viewers can identify with Jun's characters. It is no surprise that he won this year's Academy Award for best director.

a. The first paragraph explains what the person is doing today. Underline the topic sentence.

Second paragraph

> Jun has been directing films since he was 18. He directed many short movies in college, and after graduating, he won a nationwide film contest. The money he received allowed him to move to Los Angeles and enter a film school. While he was there, he was further recognized by a famous director, who said, "We'll have to keep our eye on Jun. He has great potential." Three years after graduating from film school, Jun directed his first major movie, and he has been in demand ever since.

b. The second paragraph explains Jun-Ho's rise to success. Underline the topic sentence.

Third paragraph

> Jun-Ho has two characteristics that have helped make him a great director. First, he is very intelligent and studies hard. His school grades were excellent, and he reads constantly. He can always be found with a book or magazine in hand. Second, he is a good observer. He often notices things that other people do not. For example, he is usually the first to notice when someone is sad, and he is always willing to listen to that person's problem. Because of these two important characteristics, Jun-Ho is able to make movies that are deep and insightful.

c. The third paragraph talks about characteristics that helped Jun-Ho become successful. Underline the topic sentence.

2. Your magazine article will have paragraphs similar to the first, second, and third paragraphs of the example.

Write a topic sentence for each paragraph. Then list facts or examples to support your topic sentences.

Paragraph 1: what this person is doing today

Topic sentence: _____

Facts or examples: _____

_____

_____

Paragraph 2: the road to success

Topic sentence: _____

Facts or examples: _____

_____

_____

Paragraph 3: characteristics that led to success

Topic sentence: _____

Facts or examples: _____

_____

_____

3. Now write a magazine article based on the interview with your partner.

4. When you finish writing, complete this checklist.

Self-editing checklist ☑

- ☐ *Is the first word in each paragraph indented?*
- ☐ *Does each paragraph have a topic sentence?*
- ☐ *Are the topic sentences supported by facts and examples?*

In your writing, you can use someone else's exact words. These words must be put inside quotation marks. When you do this, you are using **direct speech.**

   "The key to reaching my goal," says Jun-Ho, "is a lot of hard work."

You can make your own sentence that includes someone else's words. When you do this, you are using **indirect speech.**

   Jun-Ho says that the key to reaching his goal is hard work.

Notice that in **indirect speech** *the pronouns and verb forms change.*

1. Read the paragraph below. Then change the exact quotes from direct speech to indirect speech.

   Sally Corlin's success is due to her hard work. Her store, Sally's Sweet Necessities, specializes in creating beautiful gift baskets. Corlin explains, "It's my job to know the tastes of my customers." Corlin also makes an effort to find out what's going on in her customers' lives. She says, "I always ask them about their kids, so they see that I'm really interested." She enjoys speaking with people and always tries to delight her customers. Because she works so hard, her store has become very popular. "It's my favorite place to shop," claims regular customer Frank Wang. "I recommend Sally's to all my friends," he added.

Sally Corlin explains that _it's_____ .

She says that _____

_____ .

Frank Wang claims that _____ .

He adds that _____ .

2. Now look at the article you wrote in Lesson 6. Try to add one example each of direct speech and indirect speech to your composition. Write them here.

   Direct speech: _____

   Indirect speech: _____

What do you think?

1. Exchange the article you wrote in Lesson 6 with a partner. Read your partner's article and follow the instructions below.

a. Fill in the blanks.

article about _____ written by _____
(name)   (name)

b. Circle the phrase that describes the best point of the article.

creative writing style   written about an interesting person
easy to understand   heartwarming topic

c. Write another reason why you like the article.

_____

_____

d. Which paragraph did you like best? Why?

I liked paragraph number ___ best because _____

_____ .

2. Write a short letter to your partner. What did you like best about his or her article? Do you agree with the author's opinions? What else could the author add to the article to make it better?

Dear _____ ,

    I read your article about _____
and thought it was very interesting.

3. Exchange letters with your partner. What is one thing you learned from your feedback letter?

1. Read these important tips on writing a resume.

- Make the most important information easy to see.
- Keep the language clear and simple.
- Be sure the resume is easy to read.
- List your job and education history in reverse chronological order.
- Don't write "Resume" on the page.
- Be certain there are no spelling errors.
- Type the resume.

2. Read Laura Pei's resume below. How are resumes different in your country?

LAURA PEI
205 East Mountain Lane
Denver, Colorado 21212   USA
(303) 555-9447

OBJECTIVE
To obtain a position as a graphic designer

PROFESSIONAL EXPERIENCE
P & G Designs, Denver, Colorado, *1999–present*
Receptionist and Administrative Assistant
- Assist designers
- Work with both artists and clients
- Organize projects and filing system

Vitamin Quota, Boulder, Colorado, *1997–1999*
Sales and Stock Clerk
- Worked part-time and during holidays
- Handled cash register accounts and special orders

EDUCATION
Bachelor of Fine Arts, University of Colorado, *1999*
Clayton High School, *1995*

SPECIAL SKILLS
Extensive experience in desktop publishing
Fluent in Chinese (Mandarin)

AWARDS
Winner of Colorado Art Designer's Award, *1999*

---

3. Now write your own resume.

Unit 4 *Invent!*

Lesson 1 Everyday objects

Brainstorming

1. What are some objects that you use to make your life easier? How are they used? Brainstorm for three minutes and make two lists.

Objects	Uses
vacuum cleaner	
laptop computer	

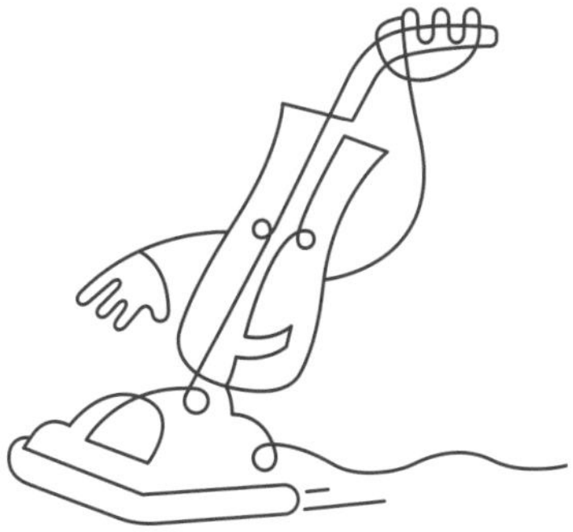

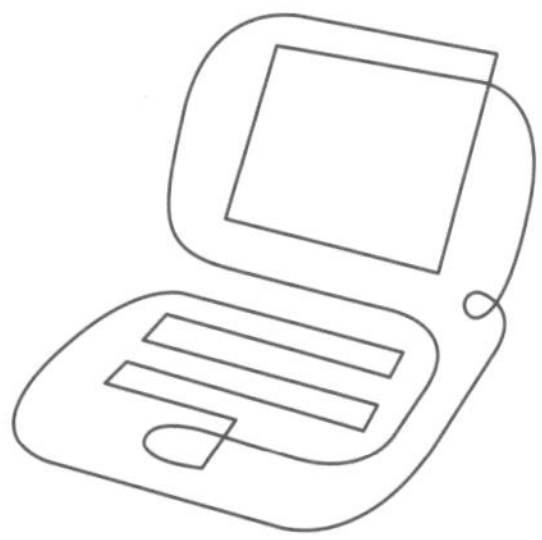

2. Now brainstorm with your class. Say your ideas for objects out loud, and your teacher will write them on the board.

3. Look at the list your teacher wrote on the board. Choose two objects from the list, and write them below. Why are they useful? How do you use them?

_______________ _______________

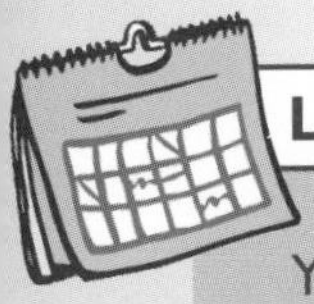

Later in this unit . . .

You will write about an invention to make life easier.

You will also learn about definition paragraphs, attention getters, and avoiding repetition.

1. Read the paragraph below and follow the instructions.

What is it?

Are you ready for a game? Here are the characteristics of a "mystery item." Can you guess what it is? It is something a lot of people use every day. In fact, many people, especially Americans, say they cannot survive without one. People rub them on the outside with special liquids so that they stay bright. The inside is sometimes filled with music from a radio, a cassette player, or a CD player. Some people even put telephones inside. They come in different colors, shapes, and sizes, but they all have two things in common. First, they have windows and four black round things on the bottom. Second, they need people to control them.

a. What is the mystery item? Write it here.

_____

b. What clues were most helpful? Write them here.

_____   _____

> **By the way,**
> this paragraph is called a "definition paragraph." Use this style when you want to tell the what, where, when, and how of something.

2. Now it's your turn. Think of your own mystery item. It should be something your classmates are very familiar with. Write clues, but don't make them too obvious.

My mystery item: _____

Clues: _____

_____

_____

_____

_____

_____

_____

3. Read your clues out loud one at a time. After each clue, give your classmates time to guess your mystery item. Did you fool the class?

A topic sentence is important because it tells the reader what the paragraph is about. It is often the first sentence in a paragraph, but not always. Sometimes the first sentence is an "attention getter." It gets the reader interested in the topic.

1. Look back at the example paragraph in Lesson 2. What word in the first sentence gets your attention? Write it here.

_____

2. Complete this chart with an attention getter for each given topic. Then choose your own topic, and write an attention getter and a topic sentence.

Topic	Attention getter	Topic sentence
Shoes	*The shoes you choose in the morning can affect your mood for the rest of the day.*	There are basically four types of shoes.
Cameras	*How can you make your special memories last forever?*	A camera records your experiences.
Health		Good health depends on good habits.
Candles		Candles are becoming increasingly popular because they can be used in a variety of settings.
Recording		Some people still choose to buy LP records rather than CDs because they say they like the look, feel, and sound of them.
(your own topic)		

3. Write an attention getter about the mystery item you chose in Lesson 2.

_____

_____

Be an inventor

1. Look at these sample inventions. What are they used for? Who do you think would use them?

| Bathing suits with safety air bags | Dishes that don't need washing | Insta-English dictionary ring |

2. Now it's your turn to invent something. Draw a picture of your invention and name it. Label the parts and write what they do.

1. Describe your invention from Lesson 4. What does it do? Make some notes.

_____

_____

_____

2. How do you use the invention? Write down the necessary steps.

First, _____ .

Second, _____ .

Next, _____ .

Then, _____ .

Finally, _____ .

3. Tell a partner about your invention. Does he or she have any suggestions for improving it?

4. Write a topic sentence that includes the name of your invention and what it does.

_____

_____

5. Now write an attention getter for a composition about your invention.

_____

_____

1. You are going to write a composition about your invention. First, read the example composition and follow the instructions.

> *The Insta-English Ring*
>
> Do you wish you could speak English better? If so, then here is the solution to your problem – the Insta-English Ring. Easy to use and effective, the Insta-English Ring is an excellent aid for English study.
>
> The Insta-English Ring is a special device that gives you English fluency. It looks like an ordinary gold ring, but it is really a small computer. This amazing language tool is made out of metal, but it can be adjusted to fit almost anyone's finger.
>
> The Insta-English Ring is easy to use. All you need to do is put it on one of your fingers. Then push the button and a tiny compartment will open. Choose the type of English you wish to acquire. The current choices are British English, North American English, and Australian English. After you make your choice, the ring sends English vocabulary and grammar up through your arm to your brain. After a few days, you will begin to notice the results. Soon, you will be speaking, even dreaming, in English.

Introductory paragraph

Second paragraph

Third paragraph

a. The first paragraph is the introduction. Circle the attention getter. Underline the topic sentence.

b. The second paragraph explains what the invention is and what it does. Underline the topic sentence.

c. The third paragraph explains how to use the invention. Underline the topic sentence.

2. In Lesson 5, you wrote a topic sentence for your first paragraph. Now write topic sentences for your second and third paragraphs.

Paragraph 2: _____

_____

Paragraph 3: _____

_____

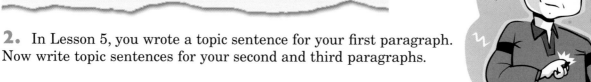

3. Now write a composition about your invention. Use your notes from Lesson 5.

4. When you finish writing, complete this checklist.

Self-editing checklist ☑

   ☐ *Do you have an introduction with an attention getter?*
   ☐ *Are your topic sentences written in a clear and interesting way?*
   ☐ *Did you use transition words to make the organization clear?*

Instead of repeating the same noun in a second sentence, use a pronoun instead.

(not good) **The Insta-English Ring** is easy to use. Just put **the Insta-English Ring** on your finger.

(better) **The Insta-English Ring** is easy to use. Just put **it** on your finger.

You can also use another word or phrase instead of repeating the same noun.

The Insta-English Ring is easy to use. **This amazing language tool** fits on your finger.

Instead of repeating a word, cross it out if it is not necessary.

The **Insta-English Ring** contains a small ~~Insta-English~~ computer.

1. Read the paragraph below. Look at each place *the memophone* is used, and decide whether you can make one of the changes above. Write any changes directly above *the memophone*.

The memophone is a device designed to send short memos.
~~The memophone~~ **It** is a box that plugs right into your telephone.
Inside **the memophone** is a microphone, computer chip, and mini-fax. As you speak to someone on the telephone, **the memophone** listens to what you say. Anytime you tell someone to do something, **the memophone** records your words and sends them as a fax to the other person's telephone. Thanks to **the memophone**, the other person will receive a written note to remind him or her what to do. **The memophone** will keep printing out the same note every day until that person pushes **the memophone's** "Done" button. **The memophone** also has "Level of Importance Sensors," too. If your voice sounds urgent, **the memophone** will print the message in red ink instead of black, and **the memophone** will send it once an hour instead of once a day. For example, if you call your husband and say, "You forgot to pick up the dry cleaning yesterday. Please, please, don't forget today!" **the memophone** will immediately print out a red memo saying, "Pick up laundry today!" This time, thanks to **the memophone**, he'll probably remember.

2. Now look at the composition you wrote in Lesson 6. Would similar changes make it better?

1. Imagine that you are a member of an awards committee. You are awarding prizes for recent inventions. Follow the instructions below.

a. Work in groups of four. Exchange your composition with a classmate in another group. On your own, read and mark each paragraph of your classmate's composition with one or more of the following comments.

interesting style	easy to understand	well-organized
needs a topic sentence	hard to understand	needs more information

b. Write which paragraph you liked best and why.

I liked the one about _____ because _____

_____.

c. Now your group must award a prize for the best invention. Tell the group about the invention you have just read about. Discuss each invention and vote for the best one.

Best invention: _____

d. Give awards to the other inventions. Choose from the awards below or think of your own.

Easiest to use: _____   Most practical: _____

Most unusual: _____   Most beneficial
to society: _____

Most likely to
be popular: _____   _____: _____
                                         (your own idea)

e. Describe to the class the invention that your group chose as the best one.

2. Write a short letter to one of the inventors. Write your comments or questions about the invention.

Dear _____ ,

    I liked your wonderful invention a lot. However, I have a few questions
about it. . . .

3. Return the compositions to their authors. Were you surprised by anything in the letter you received about your invention?

1. Keep these tips in mind when you're writing a letter to a company about a product.

- Introduce yourself.
- Give some background information.
- State your question, problem, or note of appreciation.
- Close your letter by thanking the reader.

2. Read the e-mail message below. Would you ever write a letter like this? Why or why not?

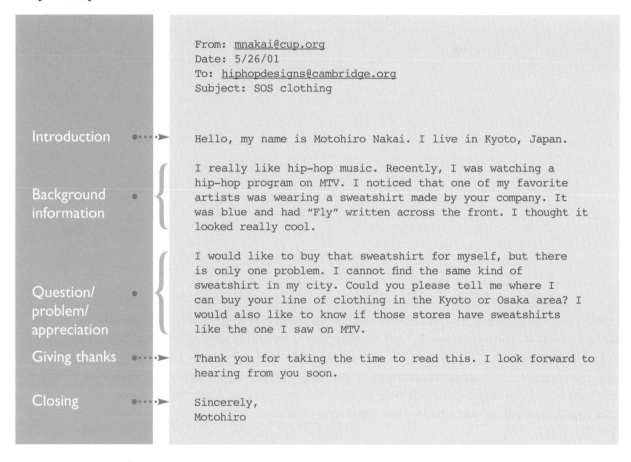

From: mnakai@cup.org
Date: 5/26/01
To: hiphopdesigns@cambridge.org
Subject: SOS clothing

Introduction

Hello, my name is Motohiro Nakai. I live in Kyoto, Japan.

Background information

I really like hip-hop music. Recently, I was watching a hip-hop program on MTV. I noticed that one of my favorite artists was wearing a sweatshirt made by your company. It was blue and had "Fly" written across the front. I thought it looked really cool.

Question/ problem/ appreciation

I would like to buy that sweatshirt for myself, but there is only one problem. I cannot find the same kind of sweatshirt in my city. Could you please tell me where I can buy your line of clothing in the Kyoto or Osaka area? I would also like to know if those stores have sweatshirts like the one I saw on MTV.

Giving thanks

Thank you for taking the time to read this. I look forward to hearing from you soon.

Closing

Sincerely,
Motohiro

3. Now write your own letter asking a question, stating a problem, or expressing appreciation. Some possible examples:

- Question: *Where can I find your clothing label in my city?*
- Problem: *My new computer software doesn't work. Can you help me?*
- Appreciation: *I am very happy with your latest line of cosmetics.*

Unit 5 *It changed my life!*

| Lesson 1 | **An important event** | | **Brainstorming** |

1. What are some important events that you have experienced during your life? Brainstorm for three minutes and make a list.

Important events

birth of my child
winning a race

2. Review your ideas. Were any of the events or experiences particularly memorable? Put a star (★) next to the experiences that taught you something valuable about life.

3. Tell a partner about an experience in your life that taught you a valuable lesson. Try to explain how it changed your outlook on life. You can choose from the expressions in the box to get started, or use one of your own expressions.

gave me confidence	*made me see something differently*	*taught me about the real world*
changed my attitude	*made me appreciate something more*	*made me interested in something*

Later in this unit . . .

You will write about an important event in your life.

You will also learn about cause-and-effect words and paragraphs, and introductory paragraphs.

1. Read the paragraph below and follow the instructions.

A Night I'll Never Forget

One night, my house burned down. Although I lost many things in the fire, the experience helped me to grow up. Before the fire, I was selfish. I always complained to my mother about how small my room was or how few clothes I had. I never thought about her troubles, just my own. Then, the fire came and destroyed everything we owned. We were suddenly poor and had to borrow everything, even food. At first, I had a hard time, but slowly I began to realize that I didn't really need my old things. I just needed my family. After all, you can get new clothes anytime, but a family can never be replaced. It is true that the fire took many good things from me, but it gave me something, too. It taught me to appreciate people more than things.

By the way, this paragraph is written in a cause-and-effect style. Use this style to show how a process causes changes.

a. The words below tell about the author's experience. Number them from 1 to 5 in the order the author writes about them.

___ fire   ___ new appreciation   ___ hard time
___ selfish   ___ lost everything in fire

b. Look at the first sentence of the paragraph. It is not a topic sentence, but rather an attention getter. Why does it catch the reader's attention? Circle the reason.

It's funny.   It's rude.

It's shocking.   It's an unusual way of thinking.

c. The last two sentences in the paragraph explain the topic. However, there is another sentence in the beginning that does so in fewer words. This is the topic sentence. Underline it.

d. Group the sentences in the paragraph in this way:

- Circle all sentences that describe the author before the fire happened.
- Put a star (★) over the sentences that tell what happened to the author.
- Put a box around all the sentences that discuss how the event changed the author.

2. Compare answers with a partner.

An introductory paragraph begins a composition and often contains these three things.

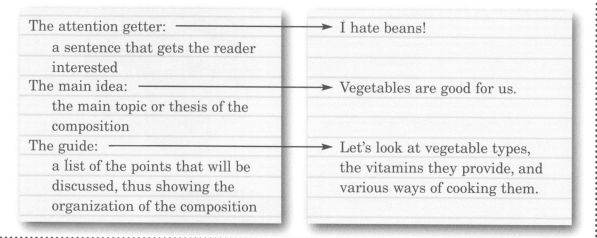

The attention getter:
    a sentence that gets the reader
    interested
	→	I hate beans!

The main idea:
    the main topic or thesis of the
    composition
	→	Vegetables are good for us.

The guide:
    a list of the points that will be
    discussed, thus showing the
    organization of the composition
	→	Let's look at vegetable types, the vitamins they provide, and various ways of cooking them.

1. Read these two introductory paragraphs from two different compositions. Then follow the instructions below.

Today I became an Australian. Although I originally came here to study for just two years, something terrible happened in my home country that made me decide to stay. In order to understand my decision, you must hear the story of my life. I will tell you about the kind of person I was before this terrible event, what happened, and how it made me decide to call this country my home.

You've been dreaming about taking a big trip for years, and the time has finally come. You know where you want to go, but the big question is whether you should go on your own or sign up for a group tour. You're thinking of going alone, but wait! This simple comparison of independent versus group tour travel might change your mind. It compares cost, safety, and use of time.

   a. In each paragraph, circle the sentence that is an attention getter.

   b. Underline the sentence that shows the main idea.

   c. Put a box around the sentence that is the guide.

2. Compare answers with a partner.

1. Look again at your brainstorming list from Lesson 1. Choose three significant events that you might like to write about.

_____

_____

_____

2. Work in groups of three. Take turns telling each other about your experiences. Ask each other questions like these:

■ How did you feel when that happened?

■ How did that event change your thinking about _____?

■ How did that event change you? What were you like before and after the event?

3. When you finish, ask your group which event they think you should write about.

4. Choose one event to write a composition about. It can be the one your group suggested or your own choice.

Write notes on how the event changed you, such as what you were like before and after the event.

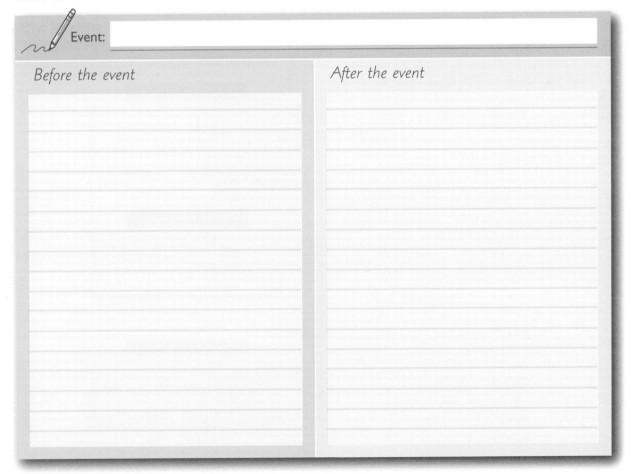

Event: _____

Before the event	After the event

You are going to write a composition with an introductory paragraph.
First, read the example composition and follow the instructions.

An Important Day

Introductory paragraph

Have you ever thought that you knew someone very well and then found out that you hardly knew that person at all? This happened to me with my father. I thought I knew him well until one day something happened that changed my attitude toward him. Let me explain how I used to see my father, what happened, and how it changed me.

Second paragraph

As a child, I was always closer to my mother than to my father. As is traditional in Japanese culture, it was my mother's job to take care of me. She fed me and played with me every day. On the other hand, I hardly ever saw my father. He would often work until late at night, and he didn't talk to me much when he came home. He got angry at me sometimes, too. I thought he was a tough, cold man, and I was a little afraid of him.

Third paragraph

Then one day, my mother got sick. My father came home from work to take care of her and told me to go to the drugstore to get some medicine. When I returned, I took the medicine to my parents' bedroom. I looked in quietly before entering and saw my mother lying down with her eyes half-closed. My father was kneeling on the floor next to her, slowly and patiently feeding her some soup. When she finished, he put the bowl down and softly kissed her forehead. On that day, I realized that my father was really a kind and loving man.

Fourth paragraph

From then on, I saw only kindness and caring in my father's eyes. As a result, I learned two important things. First, I learned that even though my father seemed rough, he was a kind man. Second, I learned that one must be very careful not to judge people. A person might look hard on the outside, but be quite different on the inside.

a. The first paragraph is the introductory paragraph. Circle the attention getter, underline the main idea, and put a box around the guide.

b. The other paragraphs follow this order:

before the event
(what I used to be like)

the event
(what happened)

after the event
(how I changed)

Decide the order in which you will write about these three topics in your own composition.

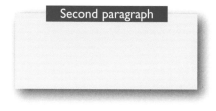

Second paragraph

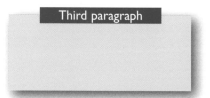

Third paragraph

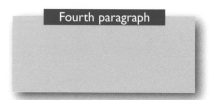

Fourth paragraph

My big event

1. Write an introductory paragraph for your composition about an important event in your life. Include an attention getter, the main idea of the composition, and the guide.

2. Look back in Lesson 5 at the order you chose for your paragraphs. Write topic sentences for your second, third, and fourth paragraphs.

Paragraph 2: _____

_____

Paragraph 3: _____

_____

Paragraph 4: _____

_____

3. Now put the parts together and write a four-paragraph composition.

4. When you finish writing, complete this checklist.

Self-editing checklist ☑

☐ *Do you have an introduction with an attention getter, main idea, and guide?*

☐ *Is it clear how the experience changed you?*

☐ *Have you read your composition again and checked your spelling?*

These cause-and-effect words are used with a noun or noun phrase.

due to   Many people became homeless **due to** the flood.
because of   The store was crowded **because of** the sale.

These cause-and-effect words are used within a sentence to show a relationship between clauses.

because   I passed the test **because** I studied very hard.
since   **Since** I forgot my money, Daniel paid for lunch.
so   The bus never came, **so** I had to take a taxi home.

These cause-and-effect words are used at the beginning of one sentence to show its relationship to the sentence before it.

as a result   Ten inches of snow have fallen. **As a result**, all roads are closed.
therefore   Dr. Marshall is sick today. **Therefore**, his speech will be delayed.

1. Rewrite these sentences using the word or words in parentheses.

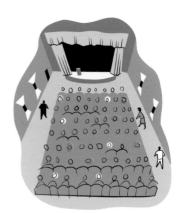

   a. There's a large crowd of people. There is nowhere to sit.

     (because of) _There is nowhere to sit because of the large_
       crowd of people.

   b. The economy is getting worse. Few companies are hiring

     workers. (therefore) _____

     _____

   c. I quit my job. I want to be a full-time professional musician. (because)

     _____

   d. There was a car accident when he was thirty. My father could not walk. (due to)

     _____

   e. My aunt often scolded me. I didn't like her very much. (since)

     _____

   f. My sister and I could not agree. We argued over little things. (as a result)

     _____

   g. My family moved to a foreign country. I learned a new language. (so)

     _____

2. Now read the composition you wrote in Lesson 6. Can you use any of these words to show cause and effect?

1. Get into groups of four. Exchange your composition with a classmate in another group. Read your classmate's story and follow the instructions below.

a. Evaluate the parts of the introductory paragraph. Check (✔) the word that best describes each part.

Attention getter	☐ missing	☐ weak	☐ good	☐ I'm not sure
Main idea	☐ missing	☐ weak	☐ good	☐ I'm not sure
Guide	☐ missing	☐ weak	☐ good	☐ I'm not sure

b. Circle one or two expressions that best describe this composition. You can add your own expressions.

heartwarming   *easy to understand*   _____

intriguing   *well-organized*   _____

c. Exchange compositions with others in your group until you have read them all. Which one do you like best? As a group, choose your favorite composition and put a star (★) on it. Then give it to your teacher.

d. The authors with stars on their papers will read their compositions to the class. After each author finishes, write a "Lesson of Life," like the ones below, that you think fits the story.

Lessons of Life
✓ Appreciate your family.
✓ Don't give up too soon.
✓ Learn from your mistakes.

2. Compare your "Lessons of Life" with a partner. Are your ideas similar?

1. Do you often give greeting cards to friends and family members? If so, on what occasions?

2. Here are some common types of greeting cards. Can you think of any other occasions when you might give a card?

| birthday | thank-you | _____ | _____ |
| anniversary | get well (soon) | _____ | _____ |

3. Look at these greeting cards. Which one do you like the most? Why?

Congratulations!

You've studied hard
And learned many things –
The gift of knowledge
Is the gift of wings.

Now that you're gone,
And though we're apart,

You'll always be near,
As near as my heart.

Someone I disliked
I looked at again,
And once I understood him,
He became my best friend.

4. You are going to design your own greeting card. Answer these questions.

a. Who are you going to give your card to? _____

b. What type of card will it be? _____

c. What "Lessons of Life" will you include? You may want to look back at your notes from Lesson 8 for ideas. Write them here.

_____

_____

5. Now design your card. Don't forget to give it to the person!

Unit 6 Exciting destinations

Brainstorming

1. What are some places you've visited? What did you do on those trips? Brainstorm for three minutes and make two lists.

Places	What I did there
Paris	museums, people-watching, boat ride on the Seine River, Eiffel Tower
India	Taj Mahal, elephant ride, spice markets

2. Put stars (★) next to the places and activities that were the most memorable.

3. When you finish, compare your travel experiences with a partner.

Later in this unit . . .

You will write about traveling.

You will also learn about process paragraphs, guidebook styles, and modifiers.

1. Read this paragraph written in guidebook style, and follow the instructions.

Making the Most of Your Trip

    Imagine standing under Big Ben or walking through Piccadilly Circus. London has so many interesting places to visit that even if you went for a week you couldn't see everything. To see as much as you can during your visit, you must plan your trip carefully. First, you should gather information about London. You can go to the travel section of a bookstore, visit a travel agency, or surf the Web for information. Next, make a list of the things you would like to do the most. For example, if you have always wanted to see the Crown jewels, then plan a visit to the Tower of London. After that, look at a map to learn about the underground train (or "Tube") lines so that you will know how to get around. Finally, write down your travel plans on a piece of paper and carry it in your pocket. Refer to it while you are there so that you won't miss anything. In conclusion, there is a lot to see in London, so take the time to plan your visit beforehand.

By the way, this paragraph uses a "process" style of organization. Use this style when you want to tell a reader how to do something.

a. Put a star (★) over the attention getter.

b. Underline the topic sentence.

c. Write one to three words below telling what each subtopic of the main topic is about.

    gather information _____   _____

    _____   _____

d. Circle the four transitional time phrases that show you when a new subtopic is beginning.

2. Compare answers with a partner.

Making a strong suggestion

If you go to San Francisco,   *be sure not to miss the Golden Gate Bridge.*
you must see the Golden Gate Bridge.
a visit to the Golden Gate Bridge is a must.
it's essential that you see the Golden Gate Bridge.

Making a weaker suggestion

While you're in Barcelona,   *you should take a walk down Las Ramblas.*
try to visit Las Ramblas.
you might want to see Las Ramblas.
it would be a good idea to visit Las Ramblas.

1. Give suggestions about the following places. Decide whether you want to make a strong suggestion or a weaker one. Use the patterns in the box above.

a. Paris / the Louvre

   If you go to Paris, _____

b. Tokyo / Meiji Shrine

   _____

c. Sydney / Bondi Beach

   _____

d. London / Buckingham Palace

   _____

e. Egypt / the pyramids

   _____

f. New York / Central Park

   _____

g. Peru / Machu Picchu

   _____

2. Now write two suggestions about your hometown or capital city.

   _____

   _____

3. Compare answers with a partner.

1. Look at the map below. Which cities have you visited or read about? Which city would you most like to visit?

2. You are going to plan a one-day itinerary in a popular tourist city. Choose the city and write its name here.

_____

3. To make your itinerary, find magazine articles or a tour book about your city. Collect information on any of these topics:

hotels	sights to see	shopping
restaurants	cultural events and festivals	customs

4. Later, when you write your composition, you will have to include a list of the sources (the names of the magazines or books you used). Look at these examples and pay attention to the punctuation.

Book				
Author Noble et al.	**Book title** _Mexico._	**City of publication** Berkeley, California:	**Publisher** Lonely Planet,	**Year of publication** 2000.
Magazine				
Author Lansing, D.	**Article** "48 Hours in Vegas."	**Magazine title** _National Geographic Traveler_	**Publication date** (July/Aug. 1999):	**Page numbers** 73–84.

5. Make a list of your sources. Be sure to include all important information.

Write a schedule for your one-day tour. Imagine that the questions below will be asked by the people on your tour. Can you answer their questions?

- *What hotel are we staying at?*
- *What restaurants are we eating at? when?*
- *When and where will the tour start? finish?*
- *What sights will we see?*
- *When and where can we shop?*
- *Are there any cultural events happening?*

Itinerary		_____ Day Tour
		(city name)
A.M.	7:00	
	8:00	
	9:00	
	10:00	
	11:00	
P.M.	12:00	
	1:00	
	2:00	
	3:00	
	4:00	
	5:00	
	6:00	
	7:00	
	8:00	
	9:00	
	10:00	
	11:00	
A.M.	12:00	

A guidebook article

1. You are going to write a guidebook article about the one-day tour you planned. First, read the example article and follow the instructions.

A Day in Vegas

Introductory paragraph

Can you visit Las Vegas and not gamble? Absolutely! Here's a one-day tour in which you won't enter a casino even once. You'll start the day with a visit to a unique shopping center, then go to a first-class restaurant, and finally end the tour next to a sinking ship.

Second paragraph

After a restful night in the Flamingo Hilton, we are ready to start our tour. Go out the front door of the hotel and you'll see the beautiful Caesar's Palace Casino across the street. Next door to it are the Forum Shops, America's most unusual shopping mall, where your tour begins. Interesting shops sell everything from refrigerator magnets to cowboy wear, and the buildings are designed to look like ancient Roman buildings. In addition, an artificial sky on the ceiling changes from sunrise to sunset once an hour.

Third paragraph

Shopping will make you hungry, so you should find a place to eat. I suggest Bernoulli's. It's not expensive and has the best Italian food in Vegas! A couple of appetizers and some pasta followed by a cup of cappuccino will be more than enough to satisfy you.

Fourth paragraph

Now, it's time for adventure. Walk down the main street, or "The Strip," to the lake in front of the Treasure Island Casino. You will see an amazing show. Two full-sized sailing ships, complete with a live crew, will sail out onto the lake and fight a battle. One of the ships is a pirate ship, the other a British vessel. At first, the pirate ship will catch fire, and it will look like the British will be victorious. Then, one last lucky shot will hit the British ship. It will explode and sink right in front of you!

Concluding paragraph

Finally, as you go to sleep, memories of a wonderful day will flash through your head: the sites of ancient Rome, the smell of delicious pasta, and the sound of cannon blasts. Don't spend too much time remembering, though. Tomorrow's plan is even more fantastic!

a. In the introductory paragraph, circle the attention getter, underline the main idea, and put a box around the guide.

b. The next three paragraphs are about shopping, eating, and going to a show. What topics will you write about?

Second paragraph

Third paragraph

Fourth paragraph

2. Write an introductory paragraph for your article in the space provided. Include an attention getter, the main idea, and the guide.

3. Look back at the topics you chose for your paragraphs. Write topic sentences for your second, third, and fourth paragraphs.

Paragraph 2: _____

_____

Paragraph 3: _____

_____

Paragraph 4: _____

_____

4. Now write your article using guidebook style.

5. When you finish writing, complete this checklist.

Self-editing checklist ☑

☐ Do you have an introduction with an obvious attention getter, main idea, and guide?

☐ Do you have clearly stated topic sentences for all your paragraphs?

☐ Did you use guidebook style to make your composition interesting?

☐ Have you read your composition again and checked your spelling?

A common type of modifier is the simple adjective.
The **friendly** people of Bali will welcome you with **warm** smiles and **exotic** flowers.

Another type of modifier is the participial adjective.
In Quito, Ecuador, you'll enjoy a **breathtaking** view of **snowcapped** mountains.

1. Rewrite these sentences about New York City using modifiers. Choose from the modifiers in the box, or use your own.

affordable	appetizing	bustling	busy
breathtaking	dramatic	exciting	exotic

a. New York City is known for its **skyline**.

   New York City is known for its dramatic skyline.

b. **People** walk down the **streets**.

   _____

c. **Shops** in Chinatown sell **food**.

   _____

d. Tourists love the **view** from the top of the World Trade Center.

   _____

e. Riding New York's **subway** is an adventure in itself.

   _____

f. The **nightlife** is famous all over the world.

   _____

2. Now go back to your composition. Rewrite three sentences using modifiers.

   _____

   _____

   _____

1. Work in groups of four. Pass your compositions around the group so everyone can read them. After you've read the other compositions, answer these questions.

a. Which composition uses the best guidebook style? Why do you think so?

_____

_____

_____

b. Which tour sounds the most interesting? Why?

_____

_____

_____

2. Choose one of the tours, and imagine that you are taking it. Send a postcard to the tour's author. Explain where you are, what you have done, and how you feel.

Here is how you write to request tourist information on cities and national parks in the United States.

city:

(City name) Chamber of Commerce
(City), (State) (Zip code)
(Country)

Seattle Chamber of Commerce
Seattle, WA 98107
USA

national park:

(Park name) National Park
Visitor's Center
(City), (State) (Zip code)
(Country)

Redwood National Park
Visitor's Center
Crescent City, CA 95531
USA

1. Look at this letter written by Hee-Sung Kim. Where does he live now? Where does he want to visit?

3905 South St.
San Francisco, CA 94102
April 23, 2001

Seattle Chamber of Commerce
Seattle, WA 98107

Dear Sir or Madam:

I am a Korean student of English currently living in San Francisco. Before I return home to Korea, I would like to visit your city. Could you please send me any information you have on local attractions? I'm particularly interested in visiting the Space Needle. I also want to do some shopping while I'm in Seattle and would appreciate any recommendations.

My address is:

Hee-Sung Kim
3905 South St.
San Francisco, CA 94102

Thank you for your help. I'm looking forward to visiting your beautiful city.

Sincerely,

Hee-Sung Kim

Hee-Sung Kim

2. Imagine you are going to visit the United States. Use Hee-Sung's letter as a model, and write your own letter requesting information.

3. Mail your letter and wait to see what you receive in the mail!

Unit 7 Research survey

Lesson 1 — Getting to know someone

Brainstorming

1. What questions would you like to ask your classmates about their families? their interests? their future plans? Brainstorm for three minutes and make a list.

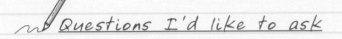

Questions I'd like to ask

How many brothers and sisters do you have?

Andy, 14

Laura, 11

Mark, 8

Mimi, 7

Jack, 4

Justin, 4

Rosie, 2

2. Compare ideas with a partner. Are there any questions you would like to add to your list?

Later in this unit . . .

You will write about your classmates.

You will also learn about classification, concluding paragraphs, and commas.

1. Read the paragraph below and follow the instructions.

Three Couple Types

How can you find out if you and your spouse are likely to be a good couple? A recent study by a psychologist might give some answers. The psychologist studied married couples to find out how people get along, and she found that there are three types of couples. The first type is the "calm-calm" couple, in which both members are calm. They almost never fight, almost never get angry, and rarely break up. In contrast, in the "passionate-passionate" relationship, both members are emotional. They often argue and sometimes have fights. However, they also tend to be more romantic and try to make up after a fight. As a result, this kind of couple is also likely to stay together. It is the third type of couple, the "calm-passionate" couple, that is most likely to break up. Because one member tends to be calm while the other is passionate, they usually have the most difficulty. Of course, not all calm-passionate couples have trouble. In some ways, they have the most interesting kind of relationship.

By the way, this paragraph uses a classification style of organization. Use this style when you want to organize information into common groups.

a. Put a star (★) over the attention getter.

b. Underline the topic sentence.

c. Circle the three subtopics in this paragraph.

d. Finish this list of transition words. What does each one do in the paragraph? Draw a line to connect each transition word to its purpose.

Transition words	Purpose
In _____	It shows a conclusion.
As _____	It shows a difference.
Of _____	It shows more information will be added to the previous point.

2. Compare answers with a partner.

3. Do you agree with the opinions in the article above? Why or why not?

Classifying people or things

You can classify people or things by organizing them into groups. When you form these groups, it's important to keep in mind who you will be writing for – that is, consider who your audience is.

1. Imagine your reading audience is fruit growers. Look at the lists below. Fruit growers need to know the kind of weather each fruit grows best in.

Audience: *fruit growers*	cool-weather fruit	warm-weather fruit	hot-weather fruit
	apples	grapes	bananas
Groups based on: *weather*	cherries	lemons	pineapples
	strawberries	limes	papayas

2. Look at these ways to classify fruits and vegetables. Add two more.

■ *by taste*　　■ *by color*　　■ *by price*　　■ _____　　■ _____

3. Imagine you are explaining fruits and vegetables to the audiences listed below. Classify fruits and vegetables into two or three groups that would best fit the audiences' interests. Be creative!

Audience: *cooks*			
	_____	_____	_____
Groups based on:	_____	_____	_____
_____	_____	_____	_____

Audience: *fashion designers*			
	_____	_____	_____
Groups based on:	_____	_____	_____
_____	_____	_____	_____

Audience: *store managers*			
	_____	_____	_____
Groups based on:	_____	_____	_____
_____	_____	_____	_____

Audience: _____ *(your own idea)*			
	_____	_____	_____
Groups based on:	_____	_____	_____
_____	_____	_____	_____

Concluding paragraphs

A concluding paragraph is the last paragraph of a composition. There are three types:

A summary repeats the main points of the composition.
A prediction discusses what will happen in the future.
An evaluation compares the main points and states what is best.

1. Which type is used for these concluding paragraphs: a summary, a prediction, or an evaluation? Write your answers in the blanks.

Concluding paragraph A   Type: _____

   In conclusion, the kinds of fruit you should use in your menu depend on the age of the person you are cooking for. Children like familiar fruits such as apples and oranges; teenagers like exotic fruits such as limes and pineapples; whereas older adults prefer berry fruits such as strawberries or cherries.

Concluding paragraph B   Type: _____

   Therefore, if you are making one meal to be eaten by people of all ages, think about their likes and dislikes. Should you use a fruit that appeals to children, teenagers, or adults? The answer is clear: to teenagers. Teenagers eat more fruit than the other groups, and they are more likely to complain about having to eat something they don't like.

Concluding paragraph C   Type: _____

   As we have seen, different age groups prefer different fruits, but what will happen in the future? Children prefer familiar fruits and teenagers prefer exotic fruits, but due to international trade and new farming techniques, the exotic fruits are becoming more familiar every day. In twenty years, teenagers will be looking for other new exotic fruits to try.

2. Compare answers with a partner.

Lesson 5 Class survey

Prewriting

1. Think of a unique research question to ask your classmates. You can use one of your questions from Lesson 1, or choose one of the questions below.

- *What kinds of clothes do you like?*
- *What is your favorite place to go to with your friends?*
- *What do you plan to do after you graduate?*
- *What problem in today's world are you most worried about?*
- *What animal would you most like to be?*
- *What would you do if you had a million dollars?*

Write your question here. ______________________________

____

2. Ask your classmates your research question. Record their names and responses on a piece of paper.

3. Next, analyze the results. Classify your classmates' answers into three, four, or five groups, using the blank chart below.

Make a heading for each group, and write your classmates' names under the appropriate group heading. Look at the example.

What kinds of clothes do you like?

Dressy clothes	**Athletic clothes**	**Casual clothes**	**Anything goes**
Keiko *Tom*	*Paolo*	*Angie* *Robert*	*Pei-Wen* *Mike*

4. Discuss the results of your survey with a partner. Are there any other ways you could classify the students using the same data?

1. You are going to write a research report based on your survey. First, read the example composition and follow the instructions.

Research Report on After-Graduation Plans

Introductory paragraph

Where will everyone be next year after they graduate? Will they return to their own countries or stay abroad? To find out, I conducted a survey. I asked each of my classmates what he or she plans to do after graduating. After looking over their answers, I realized that there are three types of students in my class: the "Don't Know" type, the "Go Back Home" type, and the "Stay Abroad" type.

Second paragraph

The group with the largest number of students, almost half of the class, consists of Don't Know types. When I asked them what they wanted to do after graduating, they got very serious and said, "I don't know," or "I haven't decided yet." In one case, a student didn't answer me at all. Another person even seemed nervous about being asked. Obviously, the members of this group are worried about their future.

Third paragraph

About a third of the students are Go Back Home types. They gave a variety of answers, but all the plans they mentioned were back in their home countries. They seemed to be a little homesick, but as soon as they talked about going home, they cheered up.

Fourth paragraph

The rest of the students — except for two that don't seem to fit any type — are the Stay Abroad types. They said they want to stay in this country or some other English-speaking country. Some want to work and some want to go to graduate school here, but none seems to want to return to live in his or her home country.

Concluding paragraph

In conclusion, the Go Back Home and Stay Abroad people have clear plans for the future, but what will happen to the Don't Know people? Will they stay here and study more, or go back home to be with their families? I think that most of them will go back. Even if they want to stay, it may not be possible.

a. The introductory paragraph explains what the writer did and his or her results. Circle these two parts of the introduction.

b. Each paragraph describes one group and explains the author's reasons for creating it. Circle the name of each group described in the second, third, and fourth paragraphs.

c. The last paragraph is the concluding paragraph. What type is used? Check (✔) one.

■ summary
■ prediction
■ evaluation

2. Look back at the groups you created in Lesson 5. Each group will be the focus of a paragraph. Write topic sentences for each of the three to five groups you made.

Paragraph 2: _____

_____

Paragraph 3: _____

_____

Paragraph 4: _____

_____

Paragraph 5: _____

_____

Paragraph 6: _____

_____

3. Write a draft of the concluding paragraph for your composition. It can either summarize or evaluate the results, or it can predict the future.

4. Now write your research report. Be sure to include an introductory paragraph.

5. When you finish writing, complete this checklist.

Self-editing checklist ☑

☐ Does your introductory paragraph explain what you did for your survey and give the results of that survey?

☐ Does each paragraph describe one group of survey participants and explain why it exists?

☐ Does your concluding paragraph either summarize, predict, or evaluate?

Read the information below on when you should use commas.

- **to list three or more things**
  Experts say that children like familiar fruits such as apples, oranges, and bananas.

- **between clauses**
  Since teenagers like exotic fruits, cooks should serve them to that age group.

- **to set off a phrase that describes**
  Berry fruits, preferred by most adults, are often used in dishes prepared for older people.

- **after certain transition words**
  In conclusion, children prefer familiar fruits.

1. Add commas to the paragraph below. The number at the end of each sentence shows how many commas to add. The first sentence has been done for you.

Campus fashions might change, but the basic college student is always the same, right? **[2]** Wrong! College students in universities all over the world have changed a lot in the last thirty years and we can expect these changes to continue. **[1]** First of all whereas college students used to be fairly young almost all aged between 18 and 22 they are now much older. **[3]** In the United States for example some reports show that there are now more college students older than 22 than younger! **[2]** In addition today's students are doing more things than before. **[1]** Thirty years ago almost all college students went to school full-time taking three or more classes. **[2]** They just studied. Today however there are more students going part-time than full-time. **[2]** They are not just studying. They are studying working and raising families. **[2]** In conclusion college students are not staying the same — they are changing. **[1]** In fact they are changing almost as quickly as campus fashions! **[1]**

2. Now look at the composition you wrote in Lesson 6. Did you use commas correctly?

1. Exchange compositions with a partner. Read your partner's composition and follow the instructions below.

a. Write the name of the research topic. _____

b. Write the groups into which the author divides the people surveyed.

_____   _____

_____   _____

c. Write what the differences between the groups are. _____

_____

_____

d. Do you agree with the author's conclusion?   *Yes*   *No*

e. Circle the phrases that best describe the composition. You can add your own phrases, too.

interesting	*useful*	*scientific*	*well-organized*
educational	*insightful*	*unique*	*thought-provoking*

2. Write a short letter to the author. Ask any questions you have about the survey or its results, and give your opinions about the research.

Dear Ying,

   Your composition was interesting and educational. I'm certainly in the minority in this class because right now I think I'm a Stay Abroad type. Although I agree with your classifications of our classmates, there is one point I disagree with. I don't think you are a Don't Know type. I think you are a Go Back Home type! Every time you speak about your country, you become so enthusiastic. I believe you are a little homesick, and I would like to talk to you about it sometime.

Sincerely,
Armando

1. As a class, make a list of local restaurants.

2. Form small groups. In your group, choose one of the restaurants you'd like to research.

3. Visit the restaurant and do these two things while you're there:

a. Pick up a sample menu or business card from the restaurant.

b. Have a meal at the restaurant. Complete the questionnaire below as a group. Write the information on an index card.

Name of restaurant:		Location:		
Type of restaurant:		Price of average main course:		
Price of average meal including drink and dessert:				
Specific ratings (circle one for each)				
Atmosphere inside of restaurant:	excellent	good	fair	poor
Quality of service:	excellent	good	fair	poor
Quality of food:	excellent	good	fair	poor
Other comments:				
Overall rating (circle one)				
★★★★ Excellent	★★★ Good	★★ Fair	★ Poor	

4. Now it's your turn to write your own review of the restaurant. Your review should focus on your own feelings and experiences.

Make some notes below. Then write your comments on an index card.

5. Collect all the cards (questionnaires and reviews) and make a class restaurant guide.

Unit 8 The power interview

1. What should you do in preparation for and during an interview? What should you avoid doing? Brainstorm for three minutes and make two lists.

DOS (things one should do)	**DON'Ts** (things one should avoid doing)
get plenty of rest the night before	look at the clock during the interview

2. What is the best thing you could do during an interview? What is the worst thing? Write them below.

Best thing: _____

Worst thing: _____

3. Now brainstorm with your class. Say your ideas out loud, and your teacher will write them on the board.

Later in this unit . . .

You will write about how to have a good job interview.

You will learn about comparison-contrast paragraphs, and expressions that show contrast. You will also be given advice on interviewing.

Analyzing paragraphs

1. Read the paragraph below and follow the instructions.

> **Two Very Different Bosses**
> Some people say that happiness at work depends on how interesting your job is, but I disagree. I think happiness depends on your relationship with your boss. I have two bosses, Michelle and Eliza, and I think Michelle is better. Michelle gives positive feedback and encourages me all the time. She makes me want to work hard and challenge myself. Eliza, on the other hand, only criticizes me. Although Michelle is very busy, she always takes the time to talk to me about my work. However, Eliza hardly ever talks to me. She keeps her office door closed with a "Do Not Disturb" sign on it. Furthermore, she doesn't allow me to make any decisions without asking her first. Michelle always trusts my decisions completely. In conclusion, whereas I dislike working for Eliza, I love working for Michelle. A good boss can make all the difference in the world.

By the way, this paragraph uses a comparison-contrast style of organization. Use this style to show how two people, places, or things are the same or different.

a. Underline the topic sentence.

b. What two things are being compared? _____ and _____

c. The three points of comparison are the subtopics. Write them below.

Main idea: _____

Subtopics: _____ _____ _____

d. Finish this list of transition words. What does each one do in the paragraph? Draw a line to connect each transition word to its purpose.

Transition words	Purpose
On _____	It shows a conclusion.
H _____	It shows a contrast.
F _____	It shows a contrast.
In _____	It shows more information will be added to the previous point.

2. Compare answers with a partner.

Expressions that show contrast

Use unlike *with a noun.*

    *Michelle, **unlike** Eliza, keeps her door open.*

Use on the other hand *and* however *with complete sentences.*

    *Eliza's door is always closed. **On the other hand**, Michelle's is always open.*
    *Eliza's door is always closed. Michelle's, **however**, is always open.*

Use whereas *and* while *to join two clauses within a single sentence.*

    ***Whereas** Michelle keeps her door open, Eliza keeps hers closed.*
    *Michelle keeps her door open, **while** Eliza keeps hers closed.*

1. Read the sentences below and write a contrasting sentence for each. Use the contrasting word or phrase in parentheses.

    a. Michelle always encourages me. (however)

       Eliza, however, never encourages me.

    b. Eliza never takes the time to talk to me. (whereas)

       _____

    c. Michelle trusts my decisions. (unlike)

       _____

    d. Eliza doesn't encourage me very much. (while)

       _____

    e. Michelle always keeps her door open. (however)

       _____

    f. I don't like working for Eliza. (on the other hand)

       _____

2. Complete these sentences with information about yourself and your classmates.

    a. Unlike my best friend, I like/don't like _____.

    b. I'm good at _____. On the other hand, I can't
       _____ at all.

    c. My favorite food is _____. However, I don't
       eat it every day.

3. Compare answers with a partner.

Interviewing for a job

1. Choose two jobs you'd like to apply for. You can choose from these examples or use your own.

newscaster	fashion model	police officer	architect	chef
teacher	waiter	baby-sitter	doctor	banker

Write your choices here.

_____   _____

2. Work in groups of three. Imagine the scene of a job interview. What kinds of questions could the interviewer ask? Brainstorm and make a list.

Interviewer's questions

Why do you want to work here?
What are some of your strengths? What are your weaknesses?

3. Now you are going to role-play. One student will be the manager (interviewer). The other two students will be applying for a job. Ask and answer questions.

Why do you want to work here?

I enjoy talking to different people, and I don't mind working on my feet.

4. After you've finished the scene, switch roles and do it again.

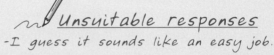

1. What are some unsuitable answers to the questions you wrote in Lesson 4? Work in groups of three. Brainstorm and make a list of inappropriate responses.

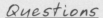

Questions

-Why do you want to work here?

-What are your weaknesses?

Unsuitable responses

-I guess it sounds like an easy job.

-I'm not good at taking orders.

-I prefer to be in charge.

2. Role-play again with an interviewer and two job applicants. This time, one interviewee should give good responses, while the other gives inappropriate responses.

Why do you want to work here?

I heard the tips are good here, and I really need the money.

3. Now perform your role-plays in front of the class. As you watch other groups perform, take notes on the DOs and DON'Ts of interviewing you see in their performance.

DOs	DON'Ts

4. Discuss as a class. Who was the best interviewee?

1. You are going to write a magazine article on good and bad interview techniques. First, read the example article and follow the instructions.

Care About What You Wear

My mother used to say, "If you want that job, dress like you already have it." First impressions are important, so wearing the right clothes to an interview can make a difference in whether or not you will get the job. There are three things you must think about when choosing clothes for an interview: color, style, and comfort.

The color of your clothes sends a message, so you should fit the clothes to the job. For example, if you are applying for a job at a bank or a law firm, you shouldn't wear bright clothing to the interview. It might make you seem immature or too wild for the job. Instead, you should wear gray, brown, or navy blue. These colors, combined with a classic white shirt or blouse, will make you seem serious.

In addition to color, the style of your suit makes a difference. A miniskirt may be attractive, but it is not appropriate in many offices. A suit that is big and baggy, or short and tight, can send a message such as "I couldn't find anything else to wear, and I don't care!" On the other hand, clothing that fits you well, without revealing too much, shows that you are neat, organized, and interested in your appearance. You must find clothes with the right fit.

The last important point about choosing an outfit is whether or not it is comfortable. If you feel comfortable and relaxed, you will look confident and capable of doing good work. However, if your clothing is too heavy or tight, you'll feel uncomfortable and nervous, and you'll look insecure. Therefore, try to wear comfortable clothes.

In conclusion, wearing the right clothes may not always get you your dream job, but my mother's advice is worth thinking about. She said that when going for an interview, your chances of getting the job are a lot better if you dress for success.

Introductory paragraph

Second paragraph

Third paragraph

Fourth paragraph

Concluding paragraph

a. In the introductory paragraph, circle the attention getter, underline the main idea, and put a box around the guide.

b. The second, third, and fourth paragraphs give suggestions for a good interview. Underline the topic sentence in each paragraph.

2. Write an introductory paragraph for your article. Include an attention getter, a main idea, and a guide.

3. Look at your DOs and DON'Ts lists in Lesson 5. What are the three most important hints for a successful interview? Write topic sentences for each of your suggestions.

Paragraph 2: _____

_____

Paragraph 3: _____

_____

Paragraph 4: _____

_____

4. Write a concluding paragraph for your article.

5. Now put the parts together, and write a composition.

6. When you finish writing, complete this checklist.

Self-editing checklist ☑

    Do you have an introductory paragraph with an attention getter, a main idea, and a guide?
    Does each paragraph have an engaging topic sentence?
    Are the DOs and DON'Ts clearly stated in your article?

When giving advice, it is important to think about the strength of the expression you choose.

strong	somewhat strong		weak
must must not	had better had better not	should/ought to shouldn't	may want to may not want to

You **must not** be late for your interview.
You**'d better** wear a suit and tie.
You **may want** to have your resume professionally designed.

1. Complete the sentences about interviewing with an appropriate form of advice.

   a. You ___*may want to*___ take a practice ride to the interview location so you can see how long it takes to get there.

   b. You _____ chew gum during the interview.

   c. You _____ arrive a little early.

   d. You _____ get a good night's sleep the night before.

   e. You _____ tell too many details about your personal life.

   f. You _____ relax so that you don't perspire too much.

   g. You _____ call soon afterward to see if you got the job.

   h. You _____ ask the interviewer some questions about the job.

   i. You _____ look around during the interview.

   j. You _____ remember the name of the person who interviewed you, even if you don't get the job.

   k. You _____ turn off your cellular phone.

2. Now go back to the composition you wrote in Lesson 6. Find three sentences that give advice. Rewrite them, using expressions for giving advice.

   a. _____

   b. _____

   c. _____

What do you think?

1. Work in groups of four. Exchange compositions with the members of another group. Make a list of the interviewing advice given in each of the compositions you have.

Composition 1

Author's name: _____

Advice:

1. _____

2. _____

3. _____

Composition 2

Author's name: _____

Advice:

1. _____

2. _____

3. _____

Composition 3

Author's name: _____

Advice:

1. _____

2. _____

3. _____

Composition 4

Author's name: _____

Advice:

1. _____

2. _____

3. _____

2. With your group, decide which advice is most useful for an interview. Write your reasons in the paragraphs below.

_____ wrote that _____

_____.

This is the most useful piece of advice because _____

_____

_____.

_____ and _____ also had useful pieces of advice.

_____

_____

3. Share your answers with the class.

1. Let's test your theories! Contact two people with full-time jobs, and interview them. Ask them what they think the top three DOs and DON'Ts are in an interview. Take notes.

Name:	Name:
Position:	Position:
<u>DOs</u>	<u>DOs</u>
<u>DON'Ts</u>	<u>DON'Ts</u>

2. When you finish, use both direct and indirect speech to report back to your group.

> Mr. Jones, our school's principal, said it's important to be positive. He said that people on job interviews must be prepared. He also said, "Don't wear jeans," and that neatness is very important.

3. With your group, choose the two most interesting suggestions to present to the class.

9

Personal goals

Lesson I	**In the future**

Brainstorming

1. What would you like to change about yourself? What are your future goals? Brainstorm for three minutes and make two lists.

Changes

I want to eat less junk food.
I want to start working out.

Future goals

I want to attend medical school.
I want to become a doctor.

2. Put stars (★) next to the things that are most important to you.

3. When you finish, compare lists with a partner.

Later in this unit . . .

You will write about personal goals.

You will also learn about persuasive paragraphs, parallelism, sentence transitions, and avoiding incomplete sentences.

1. Read the paragraph below and follow the instructions.

> *The Best Way*
>
> Life is full of choices. We often choose between doing something the easy way and doing something the hard way. Unfortunately, we almost always choose the easy way because, well, it's just easier. For example, we almost always choose to do the easiest homework assignment, to take the easiest job, or to find the easiest people to talk to at a party. However, these choices are not always the best choices. Sometimes by choosing the hardest way, there is more to gain. By choosing the hardest homework assignment, we might learn more. By choosing the toughest job, we might gain a new skill. By choosing to talk to someone who seems unapproachable at a party, we might end up making a new friend. In short, the easy way isn't always the best way.

By the way,
This paragraph uses a persuasive style of organization. Use this style when you want to convince your reader of something.

a. Put a star (★) over the attention getter.

b. Underline the first sentence that tells us why we should choose the hard way instead of the easy way. It is the topic sentence.

c. Circle the concluding sentence. It restates the topic sentence in a different way.

d. Finish this list of transition words. What does each one do in the paragraph? Draw a line to connect each transition word to its purpose.

Transition words	Purpose
For _____	It shows a conclusion.
H _____	It shows a difference.
In _____	It introduces an example.

e. By repeating the same two words in three of the sentences, the author shows a strong connection to the topic sentence. What are these two words?

_____   _____

2. Compare answers with a partner.

Parallelism

Use **parallelism** *with words and phrases to achieve coherence and rhythm in writing. When words or phrases are connected within a sentence, use the same kind of grammar.*

words	(incorrect)	*I like swimming, running, and to play tennis.*
	(correct)	*I like swimming, running, and playing tennis.*
phrases	(incorrect)	*He got up, took a shower, and eats breakfast.*
	(correct)	*He got up, took a shower, and ate breakfast.*

1. Correct each sentence below. Make the sentences parallel in structure.

a. A computer can be used to search the Internet, writing reports and letters, and to keep in touch with friends via e-mail.

A computer can be used to search the Internet, to write reports and letters,

and to keep in touch with friends via e-mail.

b. Last night I saw a movie, met some friends, and call my parents.

_____

c. Penny hopes to finish school, save some money, and will start her own business.

_____

d. Mr. Potter never saw the ocean, has never been on an airplane, and has never owned a car.

_____

e. Before you leave, please turn off the lights, water the plants, and to lock the door.

_____

f. Sam McCarthy is a doctor, writer, a husband, and father.

_____

g. The new City Arts Center is modern, functional, and looks beautiful.

_____

h. Max was a successful director, the winner of many awards, and he acted onstage.

_____

2. Compare answers with a partner.

*Good writers try to make one sentence flow smoothly into the next.
One way to do this is to start a sentence with the same idea that
ended the previous one.*

(weak transition) People in my country prefer **spicy foods**. A good example is **curry**.

(good transition) People in my country prefer **spicy foods**. **Curry** is a good example.

1. Read each pair of sentences. Then rewrite the second one so that the sentence transition is smooth.

a. I sent invitations to all my friends. The first to reply were Bess and Johnny.

  Bess and Johnny were the first to reply.

b. I'm going to Mexico this fall. The best time to visit is October.

  _____

c. The guests at the party included three movie stars. The most famous was Sean Connery.

  _____

d. Charles hopes to attend a prestigious university. His first choice is La Sorbonne in Paris.

  _____

e. Next weekend I will see several old classmates. The people I am most anxious to see are Hae-won and Peter.

  _____

f. We must study global issues. One of the most important is world peace.

  _____

g. This year, I plan to learn how to use a computer. My first task will be to send my brother an e-mail message.

  _____

h. Carrie often travels to southern Europe. Her favorite countries are Spain and Italy.

  _____

2. Compare answers with a partner.

1. Make a list of goals you want to achieve in your lifetime. Look back at your brainstorming list in Lesson 1 for ideas.

Problems I want to solve

I need to get along better with my sister.
I want to learn how to speak English fluently.

_____

_____

_____

Weaknesses I want to get rid of

I wish I were more patient.
I need to be more outgoing.

_____

_____

_____

Things I want to do

I want to climb Mount Everest.
I'd love to visit London.

_____

_____

_____

Skills I want to gain

I hope to figure out how to use a computer.
I wish I knew how to drive.

_____

_____

_____

---

2. Choose three goals and write them in the boxes below. Then set a deadline for achieving each goal.

Goal 1	Goal 2	Goal 3
_____	_____	_____
_____	_____	_____
_____	_____	_____
Achieve by:_____	Achieve by: _____	Achieve by: _____

You are going to write a letter to yourself concerning your goals. First, read the example letter and follow the instructions.

Dear Me,

    This is a letter I am writing to myself with three goals in it. I will open this letter in five years and decide whether or not I have achieved these goals. The goals I have set for myself are to learn Mandarin, go to China, and become more organized. Now, I will explain why I chose these goals and how I plan to accomplish them.

Introductory paragraph

    First, I want to learn how to speak Mandarin. I believe that China will become an even more important nation in the future. Since we will need more interpreters, I want to begin learning Mandarin now. This year, I plan to buy a book and cassettes to learn and practice at home. Next year, I will hire a private tutor. I hope to be able to carry on a simple conversation in Mandarin within two years.

Second paragraph

    Next, I would like to go to China within the next three years. I will graduate next year and get a job. With the money I earn, I'll pay for my trip myself. To this end, I plan to open a special savings account. Every month I will put some money into this account until I have enough.

Third paragraph

    Finally, it seems that I lose or forget something every day. As a result, I waste too much time trying to make up for my mistakes. I would like to become more organized. In order to do this, I will buy a special notebook and keep it with me all the time. When I need to remember something, I will write it down. Then, every morning, just after I get up, I will review my notes. My goal is to have a notebook in my pocket the day I open this letter.

Fourth paragraph

    In conclusion, I have set three goals for myself. The third is the most difficult, but it's also the most important. Therefore, I will concentrate on that goal. In fact, unless I achieve that one, I doubt I will be able to accomplish the other two.

Concluding paragraph

a. The introductory paragraph explains what the letter is for, how its author will use it, and what the writer's three goals are. Circle the three goals.

b. The second, third, and fourth paragraphs explain the goals. Underline the topic sentence in each paragraph.

c. Now think of your three goals. Write a topic sentence for each one.

Goal 1: _____

_____

Goal 2: _____

_____

Goal 3: _____

_____

d. Write a conclusion for your composition in the space provided. It should give an evaluation of your goals.

e. Now write a letter to yourself.

f. When you finish writing, complete this checklist.

Self-editing checklist ☑

☐ *Do you have an introduction with three parts?*
☐ *Do you have a topic sentence for each goal?*
☐ *Did you include a conclusion that evaluates your goals?*

g. At the end of the unit, after your letter has been returned, you should put it in an envelope. Write these words on the front of the envelope, and put it in a safe place.

Letter to myself. Not to be opened until _____, _____.
(month)   (year)

Fragments *and* run-ons *are two kinds of incomplete sentences.*

Fragments *are sentences that are not finished. They are missing something.*

(fragment) Went to a movie.   (correct) **We** went to a movie.
(fragment) My dog with big brown eyes.   (correct) My dog **has** big brown eyes.

Fragments *can be dependent clauses. They are incomplete thoughts.*

(fragment) Because it was hot.   (correct) I opened the door because it was hot.
(fragment) After he got home.   (correct) After he got home, he made dinner.

Run-ons *are single sentences that should be divided into two or more sentences.*

(run-on) The woman wore a cap, it was too big.
(correct) The woman wore a cap. It was too big.
(run-on) I ate breakfast, then I ate lunch, and I ate dinner, and it all tasted good.
(correct) I ate breakfast, lunch, and dinner. It all tasted good.

1. Rewrite this paragraph in the space provided without fragments and run-ons.

> By the age of forty, I think I will have reached many of my goals. Because I will have spent so many years working toward them. I will have two children, a boy and a girl, I will be married to a great person. Someone who shares my ideas about life and love. We will live in a home full of books instead of televisions, and we will read every night and we'll have some pets, too. Maybe a dog and cat. My spouse and I will have good jobs, we'll be able to travel around the world with our children, but sometimes by ourselves if we take time off from our jobs. I think that when I am forty. I will be a happy person.

2. Now go back to your own composition, and correct any sentence fragments or run-ons.

What do you think?

1. Get into groups of four. Exchange letters with members of another group. Read one of the letters, and follow these instructions.

a. Rate the following parts of the letter. Check (✔) the appropriate boxes.

	poor	weak	fair	good	excellent
Introduction	☐	☐	☐	☐	☐
Topic sentences	☐	☐	☐	☐	☐
Paragraph content	☐	☐	☐	☐	☐
Conclusion	☐	☐	☐	☐	☐

b. Which paragraph did you like best? Why?

I like the one about _____ because _____

_____.

c. Now read the other three letters, and discuss all the letters as a group. Which one does your group like the best? Why?

We liked the one about _____ because _____

_____.

2. Write a short letter to the author of one of the letters. Comment on the author's goals. Give some encouraging suggestions.

Dear _____ ,

I really liked your letter and the goals you've chosen for yourself. I have a few suggestions that may help you achieve your goals.

3. Give the author your letter.

1. Find out what positive things people think about you by following the instructions below.

a

Form a circle with your classmates. Take out a piece of paper from your notebook, and write your name on the bottom.

b

Hand your paper to the person sitting on your right. You will receive a paper from the person sitting on your left. You will now have a paper with a person's name written on the bottom.

c

When your teacher says to begin, write one sentence that states a good characteristic or a quality you admire about that person. Negative comments are not allowed!

d

Fold the top down so that the next person can't see what you've written. Pass the paper to the person on your right.

e

Continue writing positive comments on the papers you receive. When you have written a sentence about everyone, you will get your paper back.

2. Read your paper.

Unit 10 *Architect*

| Lesson 1 | **Facilities for college students** | **Brainstorming** |

1. What buildings, rooms, and equipment do college students need for daily living, study, and recreation? Brainstorm for three minutes and make three lists.

Buildings

Rooms

Equipment

2. Look at your lists. Decide how you could divide your ideas into smaller groups, such as the following:

rooms for studying   *rooms for socializing*   *rooms for food preparation and eating*

3. Compare lists with a partner. How many items on your lists are the same? What different items does your partner have?

Later in this unit . . .

You will design a student dormitory.

You will also learn about organizing your ideas logically and using articles correctly.

1. Read the paragraph below and follow the instructions.

A Typical Dorm Room

Where can you find an unmade bed, books all over the floor, and empty pizza boxes next to a TV? You can find them, of course, where many college students live — in a dormitory. Student dorm rooms accommodate three aspects of a student's life: daily living, study, and recreation. Daily living refers to the time a student spends sleeping, eating, cleaning, and so on. Since the average student spends about ten hours a day on daily living activities, most of the room is filled with living-related furniture: a bed, a sink, and a dresser. Students typically spend less time studying — about three hours a day — and so the only study-related furniture is a desk. The amount of time students spend on recreation varies according to the student. Some students enjoy staying in their room to watch TV or to surf the Internet, whereas others prefer going out. Interestingly, students with TVs, stereos, and computers actually spend less time on recreational activities than students with only a TV. Although there may be slight variations, all dorm rooms contain objects that relate to these three aspects of student life.

By the way, this paragraph divides a complex topic into subtopics, similar to the paragraph on page 15. The topic of "student dorm rooms" is divided into three subtopics.

a. Underline the topic sentence.

b. Circle the three subtopics.

c. Find the attention getter. Then put a box around the three examples given in it.

d. Look at the example below. Then change the other expressions in the same way.

▨ furniture related to living *living-related furniture*_____

▨ expenses related to travel _____

▨ thoughts for building confidence _____

▨ methods for making money _____

2. Compare answers with a partner.

Dividing topics into subtopics

You can take something complex and break it down into simpler parts. Look at how these topics are divided into subtopics to make them easier to explain.

How a dorm room is used
- for daily living
- for study
- for recreation

How computers are used
- for research
- for communication
- for fun

Sources of stress
- at home
- at work
- in personal relationships

1. Divide the topics below into simpler subtopics.

Sports

Student life

Marriage

Fashion

Heroes

Types of music

2. Compare subtopics with a partner. How are they different?

1. Imagine you are an architect. Read this memo from your boss. What kinds of rooms will your dormitory building have?

To: All employees
From: The chairman
Subject: New project
Date: August 17

Please begin work immediately on our new project: a
dormitory for international students. As you make your
floor plans, keep these points in mind.

- You must include at least eight student rooms in
  your design.
- The dormitory must include shower and laundry
  facilities.
- You must design the inside rooms as well as the
  outside environment (trees, gardens, pool, etc.).

2. Look at this list of items. How would you categorize the items? Put them under the appropriate headings.

cafeteria	garden	library	sauna	student lounge
computer room	gym	pool	showers	tennis court
game room	laundry room	pond	kitchen	copy center

a related to daily living	**b** related to studying	**c** related to recreation

3. Look at the completed chart. What items would you most like to have in your dormitory environment? Join a partner and choose your favorites.

A floor plan for a new dormitory

Fill in the floor plan using the symbols below. Draw one symbol in each square of your floor plan. Don't forget to show doors and windows in the buildings.

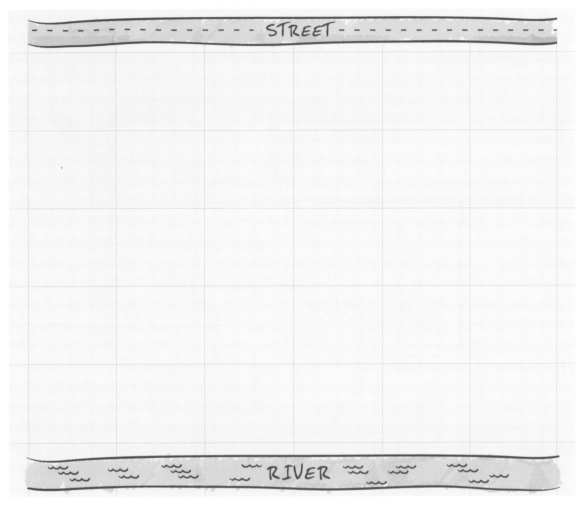

cafeteria

computer room

entrance

game room

garden

gym

kitchen

laundry room

library

pond

pool

showers

student lounge

student room

trees

1. Look at this sample floor plan for the Live Green Dormitory. Can you locate the following items? Which would you most like to visit?

- Tarzan Sports Center
- Amazon Rain Forest
- Victoria Falls Laundry Room
- Jungle Snack Bar
- Mountain Top Library
- Lake Tahoe Pond

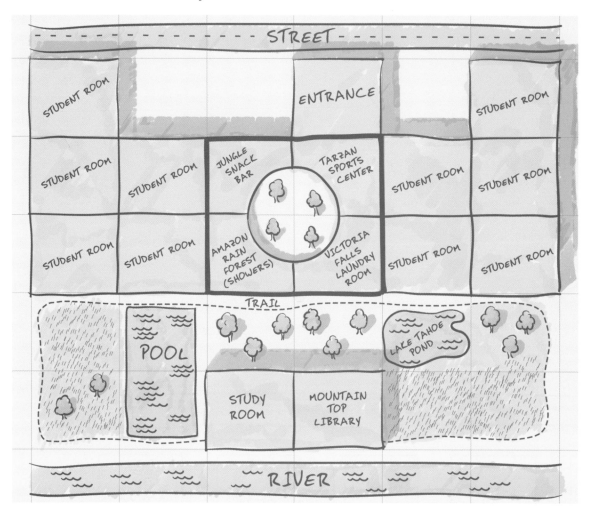

2. Read the example composition below, and follow the instructions. Use the floor plan in Exercise 1 as a reference.

Live Green

    Live Green! That's our motto, and you'll find this philosophy in our plans for the Live Green Dormitory. This dorm has been specially designed for students who enjoy being surrounded by nature. We've included our Live Green theme in facilities for daily living, study, and recreation.

    In the center of the dorm is the Greenhouse of the Americas, where students can take care of their daily needs. The greenhouse is made of four rooms: the Tarzan Sports Center, where students can exercise; the Amazon Rain Forest, where students can shower; the Victoria Falls Laundry Room, where students can do laundry; and the Jungle Snack Bar, where students can eat natural, healthy food.

    For studying, our Mountain Top Library is perfect. The glass-walled library looks out onto the surrounding gardens and contains thousands of books about nature. It also has several laptop computers connected to the Internet. Students can study while sitting in large, soft chairs and listening to birds singing softly in the background.

    Our Live Green Dormitory also has several places for recreation. The outside grounds include a trail for running. The trail goes around Lake Tahoe Pond, a beautiful pond filled with natural spring water. In addition, trees surround the large swimming pool. Students can enjoy sitting under the trees and relaxing with their friends.

    In the Live Green Dormitory, you're surrounded by nature 24 hours a day. Since we are all a part of nature, isn't living in nature the ideal way to live?

Introductory paragraph

Second paragraph

Third paragraph

Fourth paragraph

Concluding paragraph

a. In the introductory paragraph, underline the attention getter, circle the main idea, and put a box around the guide.

b. The second, third, and fourth paragraphs divide the topic into subtopics. What subtopics did the author use? Write them below.

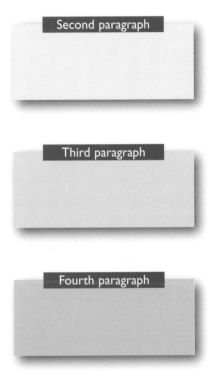

Second paragraph

Third paragraph

Fourth paragraph

3. Now write a composition about your own dorm design. Imagine that it will be read by students who are thinking of moving into the dorm. Include an introduction, three paragraphs on the dorm design, and a conclusion. Also, include your floor plan.

4. When you finish writing, complete this checklist.

Self-editing checklist ☑
    Does your composition have a clear topic and subtopics?
    Are your topic sentences clearly written?
    Did you include your floor plan with your composition?

Use **the** *when your reader already recognizes the specific person, place, or thing you are writing about.*

 I walked out of **the** *library and into* **the** *study room.*

Use **a** *and* **an** *when you are mentioning a person, place, or thing for the first time and* **the** *when you mention it again.*

 Our dorm has **a** *sports center.* **The** *sports center is free.*
  └─── first time ───┘ └─── second time ───┘

Use **a** *and* **an** *to refer to something in general. Use* **the** *to refer to something specific.*

 It's fun to be **a** *student.*
 The *student who lives next door is friendly.*

1. Add articles to this paragraph.

Let me tell you about _____*a*_____ college dormitory in Los Angeles. It's at
          a

ULA – the University of Los Angeles. Since ULA is _____ big university,
               b

_____ dorms are large and have many students living in them. Most
 c

of _____ students at ULA are from California, but some of _____
  d   e

students are from abroad. The dormitory has many suites, which are like small

apartments. _____ suites include four bedrooms with two beds each,
     f

_____ kitchen and _____ bathroom. _____ kitchen is large
 g   h   i

enough for students to cook _____ big meal. _____ dorm students really
         j   k

appreciate this because sometimes _____ cafeteria food is not so good, and
           l

they like preparing their own meals. _____ bathroom is also large and has
          m

_____ Japanese-style bathtub as well as Western showers. In addition to
 n

_____ suites, there are living rooms on each floor. Each living room has
 o

_____ big sofa, some soft chairs, and _____ large-screen television.
 p   q

Everyone says that living in a dorm at ULA is _____ wonderful experience.
             r

2. Now look at the composition you wrote in Lesson 6. Did you use articles correctly?

1. Get into groups of four. Exchange compositions with members of another group. Read one of the compositions, and follow the instructions.

a. Does the composition have an introductory paragraph?   *Yes   No*

b. What topics are paragraphs 2, 3, and 4 about?

Paragraph 2: _____

Paragraph 3: _____

Paragraph 4: _____

c. Circle the phrase that best describes this composition.

creative dorm plan   easy to understand
good choice of topics   interesting writing style

2. Write a short letter to the author. Explain what you think the design's strong points and weak points are.

3. Now read the other three compositions. Discuss them with your group members, and choose one for an award. Draw a ribbon at the top of the paper. Which composition/floor plan did you choose? Why?

1. Now that you have designed a new dorm, tell the world about it. Make a poster advertising your dorm. Uses these ideas in your poster.

- an advertising slogan
- a brief description
- various scenes of students using the dorm's facilities

- room availability information
- a list of special features
- contact information

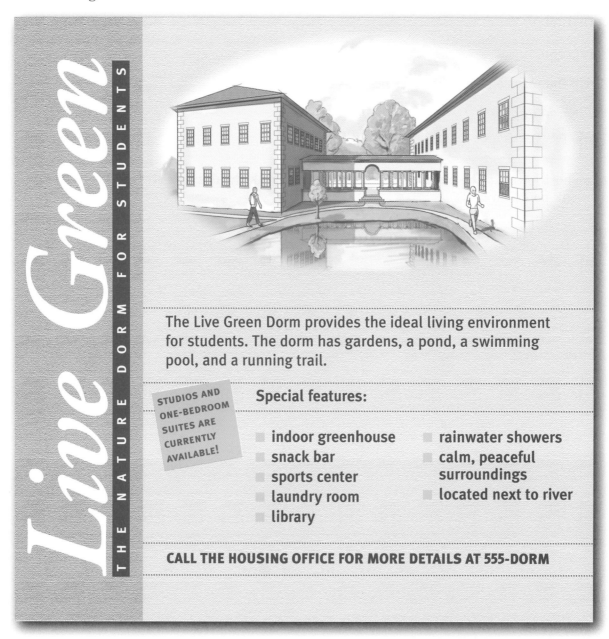

2. When you finish, hang your posters up around the classroom. Whose dorm sounds most appealing?

Lesson 1 — Important people in my life

Brainstorming

1. Who has influenced you in your life? Your parents? A teacher? A friend? Brainstorm for three minutes and make a list. You should include both people you know and famous/important people.

People

Mom
Mr. Philips - my music teacher
Beethoven - musician

2. Describe some of the people on your list to your partner. Explain why these people have had an influence on you.

Later in this unit . . .

You will write about an important person in your life.

You will learn how to link paragraphs.

You will also learn how to put topics in order and learn about subject-verb agreement.

Here are some ways of linking the last sentence of a paragraph with the first sentence of the paragraph following it.

A transition word or phrase *can be used to connect ideas between paragraphs.*

> *If I could go anywhere, it would be to Latin America.*
>> <u>First of all</u>, *I would like to visit my friend Chris in Chile.*

A word (or words) *from the last sentence of one paragraph can be used again in the first sentence of the next paragraph.*

> *If I could go anywhere, it would be to <u>Latin America</u>.*
>> <u>Latin America</u> *has a lot of places that I would like to visit.*

An idea *from the last paragraph can be used again in the first sentence of the next paragraph.*

> *If I could go anywhere, it would be somewhere in <u>Latin America</u>.*
>> <u>Chile</u> *would be my first stop.*

1. Read the sentences below. Circle the link that is used.

   a. Singing is one of my favorite hobbies.
   In fact, I hope to sing professionally someday.

   | Transition | Word | Idea |

   b. A great humanitarian was Princess Diana.
   Diana used her fame to help the less fortunate.

   | Transition | Word | Idea |

   c. I want to travel before I get a full-time job.
   I don't know what work best suits me yet.

   | Transition | Word | Idea |

   d. I knew then that Jane would agree with me.
   However, I didn't consider what Al would say.

   | Transition | Word | Idea |

2. Write two sentences about a famous person. Link them with a transition, word, or idea.

_____

_____

_____

_____

1. Read the composition below and underline the links
connecting the paragraphs.

Two can be better than one! I have two best friends.
Although they are much younger than me, we get along just
fine. We read, eat, and play together every day.

We like games. Our favorite one is "dress up." We put on
makeup and costumes in order to look like pirates, princesses,
or police officers. Then, we laugh and make funny faces. We
can spend hours pretending we're other people.

Pretending we're other people is certainly fun, but we don't
spend all of our time acting and joking. We also spend time
eating. Sometimes we eat outside in the park or at a restaurant.
It doesn't matter where we eat, as long as we do it together.

Another thing we like to do together is read. Every night
we sit and read at least two stories about characters like
Winnie the Pooh or Spiderman. Sometimes we all fall asleep
together after the last story.

In conclusion, maybe you have guessed who my special
friends are. If you haven't, I'll give you another hint. They have
lived with me since they were born. Have you guessed? My
two best friends are my children, Wes and Sofia.

2. How are the paragraphs above linked? Write *transition word, word,* or *idea.*

Paragraphs 1–2	Paragraphs 2–3	Paragraphs 3–4	Paragraphs 4–5
idea			

3. Read the introductory paragraph below.

There are many people who have had an influence on me. One of the most
important is someone I have never met, but I have seen her lovely face in many
photographs. I have heard many things about her from my parents and grandparents.
This woman, who led a remarkable life, is my great-grandmother, Rose.

4. Write the first sentence of the paragraph that might follow this introduction, using
each of the three ways of linking paragraphs.

Transition: _____

Word: _____

Idea: _____

An important person

1. Look at your brainstorming notes from Lesson 1. Choose a person to write about who has been especially important to you.

What is your relationship to this person? Choose a specific incident that shows *why* this person is important to you.

Person	Relationship	Incident

2. Tell your partner about the person and the incident.

3. Write additional details about the incident in the first box below.

Subtopic 1: _the incident_

_____

_____

Subtopic 2: _____

_____

_____

Subtopic 3: _____

_____

_____

4. Choose two other subtopics that you would like to include. Write your sentences in the boxes above. You may use the subtopics below, or make up your own.

- positive characteristics of this person
- how your life would be different without this person
- how you came to know this person
- what this person has taught you

- problems in your life this person has helped you solve
- _____

  (your own idea)

Putting topics in order

1. Read these three subtopics about Seiji, which are arranged in two different ways. Decide which one you like better. There is no one "correct" answer.

Arrangement 1	
Who	Seiji and I are in the same class. He is a quiet student but is not afraid to help others. He gives me great advice.
Problems	I write many reports for classes and sometimes don't do so well. However, if I have a friend like Seiji, I know that I can succeed.
Incident	Last year, I was working on a research paper. I thought the topic was too difficult and became discouraged. Seiji helped me and told me not to give up. I finished the paper and got the best grade in the class!

Arrangement 2	
Incident	Last year, I was working on a research paper. I thought the topic was too difficult and became discouraged. Seiji helped me and told me not to give up. I finished the paper and got the best grade in the class!
Who	Seiji and I are in the same class. He is a quiet student but is not afraid to help others. He gives me great advice.
Problems	I write many reports for classes and sometimes don't do so well. However, if I have a friend like Seiji, I know that I can succeed.

2. Now look at your three subtopics from Lesson 4. What order should they be in? Will the incident be the first, the middle, or the last?

Think of three different ways your subtopics could be arranged, and write them in the boxes below.

Arrangement 1	Arrangement 2	Arrangement 3

3. With a partner, discuss each arrangement and decide which you like the best. Circle the number of your final decision.

1. You are going to write a composition about the person you chose in Lesson 4. First, read the example composition and follow the instructions.

An Important Person in My Life

I have read the words of great thinkers and studied the acts of heroes, but none of them taught me acceptance, the most important thing in life. I learned how to accept life as it is from my father. However, he did not teach me acceptance when he was strong and healthy, but rather when he was weak and ill.

My father was once a strong man who loved being active, but a terrible illness took all that away from him. Now he can no longer walk, and he must sit quietly in a chair all day. Even talking is very difficult. One night, I went to visit him with my sisters. We started talking about life, and I told them one of my beliefs. I said that we must constantly give things up as we grow — our youth, our beauty, our friends — but it always seems that after we give something up, we gain something new in its place. Then suddenly my father spoke up. He said, "But, Curtis, I gave up everything! What did I gain?" I thought and thought, but I could not think of anything to say. Surprisingly, he answered his own question: "I gained the love of my family." I looked at my sisters and saw tears in their eyes, along with hope and thankfulness. As for me, though, I disagreed. I thought to myself, "You are wrong, Father. You always had our love. What you really gained was the power to say those words. Even in your pain, you think of others first."

I was touched by his words of acceptance. After that, when I began to feel irritated at someone, I would remember his words and become calm. If he could replace a great pain with a feeling of love for others, then I should be able to give up my small irritations. In this way, I learned the power of acceptance from my father.

Sometimes I wonder what other things I could have learned from him had I listened more carefully when I was a boy. For now, though, I am grateful for this one gift.

---

2. Write your composition. Write at least four paragraphs. Be sure to include one paragraph that explains the incident and one that concludes the composition.

3. When you finish writing, complete this checklist.

Self-editing checklist ☑

☐ Do you have at least four paragraphs, each with a clear topic?
☐ Did you link your paragraphs?
☐ Is the arrangement you chose obvious to the reader?
☐ Have you checked your spelling and grammar?

As your sentences become more complex, it becomes easier to make mistakes with subject-verb agreement. Read these rules about agreement.

When each, every, neither, and one of are used, the verb is in the third-person singular form.

> *Each person **has** his own notebook.*
> *Neither of us **is** able to come.*

When words such as someone, anything, everywhere, and nobody are used, the verb is in the third-person singular form.

> ***Is** there anything I can do?*
> *Someone **was** knocking at the door.*

Even when a verb is separated from its subject, the subject and verb must still agree.

> *The **books** that I asked my sister to bring from the library **are** overdue.*
> *The **woman** sitting on the bench feeding birds **is** my neighbor.*

1. Read the sentences below. If the verb agrees with the subject, write **OK** in the blank. If the verb does not agree with the subject, cross it out and correct it.

   a. She ~~like~~ sports. _____*likes*_____

   b. Each of the children have a toy. _____

   c. Neither of the stores that I visited today are open. _____

   d. Both of my friends are sick. _____

   e. A minivan, like other types of cars, has four wheels. _____

   f. Janet, of all my friends, are the most loyal. _____

   g. There are no problems that I cannot solve. _____

   h. One of the kindest people I know is my grandfather. _____

   i. Nobody were on the other line when I picked up the phone. _____

   j. My boss Joanna and her sister from New York are coming over for dinner. _____

   k. People from all over the world is going to be at the festival. _____

   l. No one, especially not Tim and Patricia, is allowed in before seven o'clock. _____

2. Now look at the composition you wrote in Lesson 6. Correct any similar mistakes.

1. Work in groups of four. Exchange compositions with the members of another group so that each person has one composition to review. Read the composition.

2. Circle the expression that best describes the composition. You can add your own expressions.

unusual and interesting   *warm and personal*

well-written and easy to understand   *needs more work*

_____   _____

3. Which paragraph did you like the best? Why?

I like the one about _____ *because* _____

_____

_____ .

4. Write a short letter to the author. Write either your opinions and questions, or how this arrangement compares to yours.

1. Now that you have written *about* someone who has influenced you, why don't you write a letter *to* that person and tell him or her how you feel? First, read the model below.

2. Now write your own letter.

Dear Father,

In our composition class, we were asked to write a paper about an important person in our lives. At first I couldn't decide whom to write about. Many famous people have influenced me. I've also been influenced by my best friend, Jim, from elementary school. Do you remember him? We're still friends!

In the end, however, I chose you. Enclosed is a copy of my composition about you.

I know we haven't gotten along very well recently, but I want you to know that I am grateful for all the time and love you gave me when I was growing up.

Thanks, Dad. I owe you a lot.

Love,
Curtis

3. If you like, mail your letter and composition to the person.

Brainstorming

1. What are some interesting things that have recently happened to you, your classmates, your school, or your community? Brainstorm for three minutes and make a list.

Recent events

new cafeteria opened
big windstorm

New Campus Cafeteria Opens

Big Storm Damages Area

2. Compare lists with a partner. Mark the most interesting topics with a star (★).

3. Tell the whole class the most interesting things that have happened. Your teacher will write them on the board.

4. Choose three topics from the board that you would like to write a newspaper article about. Write them here.

_____ _____ _____

Later in this unit . . .

You will write an article about a recent event.

You will also learn about newspaper article types, headlines, and using other words for *said*.

Writing for a newspaper

1. Here are three different pages you typically find in a newspaper. Which are you most likely to read? Why?

Front page	Editorial page	Society page
This page carries the most important news reports of the day.	This page contains articles and letters that give opinions about controversial issues.	This page carries articles about major social events.

2. Read these three short newspaper articles. On which page would you expect to find each one? Write your answers in the blanks.

a _____

George DeBartolo, a popular teacher at Markson High School, has decided to leave this year after twenty-five years of teaching tenth- and eleventh-grade English.

"I'll certainly miss this place," DeBartolo stated as he formally announced his early retirement, "but I need to do other things in my life!"

There will be a special ceremony on Saturday at 8:00 P.M. in the school auditorium, as DeBartolo says good-bye to all of his beloved students and colleagues.

b _____

La Maison Restaurant featured last night's retirement party for Markson High School's famous English teacher, George DeBartolo.

Guests wore clothing by top designers: Donna Karan being the overall favorite for women, Calvin Klein for men.

The celebratory formal dinner was hosted by Mayor Kelly and included such distinguished guests as Congresswomen Bloom and Bradshaw, two of DeBartolo's former students. Speakers praised DeBartolo for winning a record six "Teacher of the Year" awards over his tenure.

After being served an exquisite meal of gourmet delights prepared by La Maison's top chef, guests enjoyed dancing until almost 1:00 in the morning.

c _____

Last week, we lost another one of our best teachers, George DeBartolo. Maybe if we paid our teachers what they deserved, the good ones would not quit so often.

Though teachers are highly respected in our society, their salaries are so low that they often work at other jobs just to make ends meet. If he'd had a better salary, Mr. DeBartolo might have stayed at Markson High School.

The good-bye party for Mr. DeBartolo certainly cost a lot, but it might have been one of the only times he was rewarded for his many years of service.

We need to keep teachers like George DeBartolo. Mayor Kelly should give out more money at the beginning of their careers, rather than at the end.

3. Which article was the most interesting? Why?

1. A newspaper contains different kinds of news articles and sections.
Look at the list below. How many do you know? Which do you like to read?

a. advertisements	f. fashion news	k. news reports
b. advice column	g. financial news	l. obituaries
c. classified ads	h. home and garden	m. society pages
d. editorials	i. human-interest stories	n. sports stories
e. entertainment reviews	j. interviews	o. weather report

2. The titles of newspaper articles are called headlines.
They are short and simple.

Read the headlines below and match each to an item from
the list in Exercise 1. Some headlines may have more
than one possible answer.

1. __k__ **Missing Student Found in Alaska**

2. ____ *Mayor Kelly: Is He Fit for the Job?*

3. ____ **Toronto's 101st Annual Firefighter's Ball**

4. ____ **The Miniskirt Is Back Again**

5. ____ **Tigers Win Thrilling Finish, 3-2 in Overtime**

6. ____ **Dollar Grows Stronger This Week**

7. ____ **Your Pet Understands You Better Than Your Spouse**

8. ____ *Brad Pitt Tells All to Movie Star Magazine*

9. ____ *Jackie Chan's Latest Movie a Smash at the Box Office*

10. ____ Local Company CEO Is Dead at 59

11. ____ **Warm Temperatures for the Weekend**

12. ____ *Decorating Tips for Your Living Room*

3. Write your own headlines about a story of interest to you.

_____

_____

4. Show your headlines to a partner. Can your partner guess where in the newspaper
your headlines would be found?

Planning an article

Here are some suggestions for writing a newspaper article.

- *Think about who your readers are and their interests.*
- *In your article, answer the questions Who? What? When? Where? Why?*
- *Write a concise headline to summarize the article.*
- *Get to the point. Introduce all the major points in the first paragraph.*
- *Use active verbs like* saw *or* ran *instead of* was *or* were.

1. You are going to make a class newspaper. What would you like to write about? Choose topics from your brainstorming in Lesson 1. What style will you use for each topic?

Topic	Style
increase in cost of school uniforms	*editorial*

2. Join your classmates and discuss your different ideas. Which topics will be included in your newspaper? Assign two writers for each topic.

Topic	Style	Writers

3. Work with your writing partner. Write down your topic and make some notes about the kind of information you should include.

Topic: _____

Information to include: _____

_____

_____

_____

You are going to write a newspaper article. First, read the example article and follow the instructions.

Cindy Comes Home

After spending two years in Lima, Peru, Cindy Certello has returned to her native town of North Brookfield, Massachusetts. Soon, she will marry her high-school sweetheart and start teaching Spanish. The town celebrated her return last Thursday with a picnic.

"It's weird," said Cindy while hugging old friends. "I mean, in some ways it feels like I never left. On the other hand, I know I have changed a lot." Then, as she picked up her three-year-old nephew and kissed him on the cheek, she exclaimed, "Some of you have changed even more than I have!"

Cindy also commented, "I missed everyone here. It was hard being so far away." Adding that she was about to become a Spanish teacher at the local high school, she stated, "Now I can share my experience abroad with the whole community."

"We missed her so much," exclaimed Mrs. Certello as she wiped tears from her eyes. Then she grabbed her daughter and hugged her. "I was afraid she would stay away forever!" she cried.

"I knew she would come back," remarked Cindy's fiancé, Mark Jonas. "We said we would get married someday, but we just weren't ready two years ago. Now we are. So, last month, when I went to visit her, I took a ring along!" Mark proudly held up Cindy's hand to show us the ring. Then he added, "By this time next year, we'll be married!"

a. What type of article is this?

_____

b. Paragraph 1 answers these five questions. Fill in the answers.

Who? _____

What? _____

When? _____

Where? _____

Why? _____

c. Paragraphs 2–5 don't have topic sentences, but each is written about one topic. Write the paragraph number next to its topic.

_____ fiancé's comments

_____ changes

_____ mother's comments

_____ future plans

d. Now take notes for your first paragraph. Who will your article be about?

Who?	
What?	
When?	
Where?	
Why?	

e. What will the main topics be for the remaining paragraphs?

Paragraph 2: _____

Paragraph 3: _____

Paragraph 4: _____

Paragraph 5: _____

f. Write the first paragraph for your article in the space provided. Make sure you remember these points:

■ Think about your readers' interests.

■ Answer *Who? What? When? Where?* and *Why?* in the first paragraph.

■ Use a headline to summarize the article in a few words.

■ Use active verbs like *saw* instead of *was*.

g. Now finish your article on a separate sheet of paper.

1. What are some other words you can use instead of *said*? Look at the article in Lesson 5, and write some of the words the writer used.

_____   _____

_____   _____

2. Here is a list of words you can use instead of *said*. If you know any others, add them to the list.

admit	*claim*	*demand*	*remark*
agree	*comment*	*exclaim*	*respond*
answer	*complain*	*explain*	*state*
ask	*cry*	*inquire*	*suggest*
_____	_____	_____	_____

3. Look at these words. Which ones are used when someone is speaking loudly? speaking softly? Use a dictionary if necessary.

■ mumble   ■ shout   ■ scream   ■ whisper   ■ yell

Read the article and fill in the blanks. Use a different verb for each blank.

Residents of Canton, Ohio, were surprised yesterday to find that City Hall had been painted yellow during the night. Mayor Joan Carter _____ , "We don't know who did it or how it happened. We are looking for the mysterious painter now. But," she _____ , laughing, "it's a nice color. I like it better than gray."

Not all of the town residents agree. Gavin Wang, a dentist, _____ , "I think it's terrible. Whoever did this should be punished."

"Who did such a thing?" _____ Barbara Koh, a grocery store owner. "No building is safe anymore," she _____ . "Where were the police?" she _____ .

Police officer Mark Morris _____ , "We don't have any clues, but we're doing our best." He _____ that he had a detective working on the case.

Hadas Bori, 6 years old, was very happy to see the brightly colored building on her way to school. "It's pretty!" she _____ . "I want someone to paint my school building the same color," she _____ .

4. Now look back at your own article. Can you replace *said* with any of the words above?

1. Divide into groups according to what type of article you wrote. Exchange articles with your classmates, and read the articles. Then follow the instructions below.

a. Circle the phrase that best describes the article.

amusing   *holds your interest*

good information   *creative use of words*

simple and straightforward   *good organization*

b. Make suggestions to the author on each of these points.

1. How can the article hold the reader's interest better?	
2. Are the questions Who? What? When? Where? and Why? answered?	
3. Is the headline short and eye-catching?	
4. Are all of the main points in the first paragraph?	
5. Can any verbs be changed to active verbs?	

2. Now read the rest of the articles. Discuss them and choose the article your group likes the best.

3. Draw a ribbon at the top of the article.

Making a class newspaper

Layout and content tips

- ▪ *Put the articles in a two- or three-column format.*
- ▪ *Make sure the news stories and feature articles are interesting to the reader.*
- ▪ *Include a variety of news stories, feature articles, cartoons, illustrations/photos, advertisements, and letters to the editor.*

Typing tips

- ▪ *Use a serif typeface such as "**Times**" for your articles and a sans serif typeface such as "**Helvetica**" for your headlines.*
- ▪ *When typing on a computer, don't push* RETURN *at the end of a line.*
- ▪ *Don't use the* SPACE *bar to align text. Use* TAB *instead.*
- ▪ *Don't* underline *or use CAPITALS to emphasize. Use italics instead.*

1. Look at this model layout for the first page of a class newspaper, and study the vocabulary.

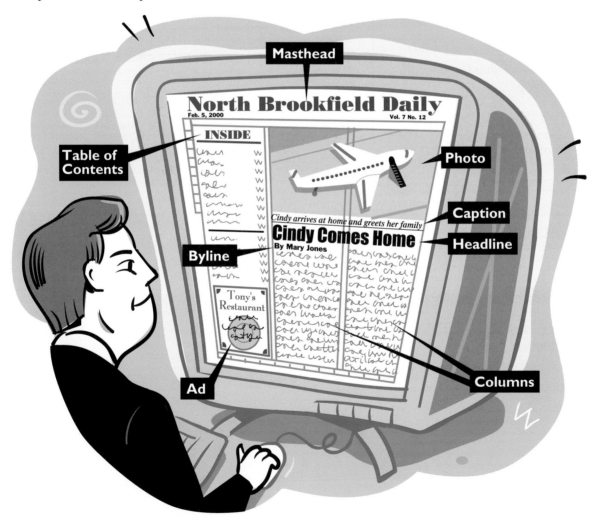

2. After studying the information above, you are ready to start organizing your own class newspaper. Good luck!

Teaching composition is not easy. Sometimes it is hard for the teacher to see things the way you do.

Give your teacher some advice so that he or she can teach this class even better next time. Choose at least three of the topics below, and write your teacher a letter.

- What you learned
- Your teacher's strengths
- What you found difficult
- The good and bad points of the class

- Your most and least favorite lessons
- A comparison to other writing classes
- What you would like to study less or more of
- How you changed from the beginning to the end

Challenge

If you have time, send us – the authors – a letter, too. We would like to know what you liked or didn't like about this book. Although we can't promise to send you an answer, we will read your letter with care.

Dear Professors Kelly and Gargagliano,